500 Miles of South Lake Tahoe Hikes

Peaks, Day Hikes, and Overnighters

Aaron M. Hussmann

DISCLAIMER

This book is only meant as an introductory guide to hikes in the South Lake Tahoe regional area. This guide book does not guarantee your safety, and you must hike at your own risk. Neither CreateSpace nor Aaron Hussmann is liable for property loss or damage, personal injury, or death that may result from accessing or hiking the trails within this book. You should be aware that hikers have been injured and killed in the Lake Tahoe area. Use caution when hiking near steep drop-offs, through boulder fields, on steep inclines, or in any terrain that may be beyond your ability level. Please read the information presented in this book carefully, especially the introduction, regarding safety and guidance while traveling through the backcountry. If necessary, seek guidance from additional sources. Spend time familiarizing yourself with the area, the terrain, and any route you plan to hike, asking questions of others when unsure. Expect unforeseen circumstances to arise, and do your best to prepare for these cases.

DEDICATION

This trail guide is dedicated to my Oma and Opa, Gunter and Christa Hussmann. My deep love for the mountains would not be possible without their bold relocation to the Tahoe basin in the 1970's, and this book would most likely not exist. I also wish to dedicate this book to my parents, Peter and Nancy Hussmann, who after a brief absence, could not resist the pull of the Sierra Nevada. With their love and support, my appreciation for these mountains has flourished.

Contents

Acknowledgements

This guidebook and the hikes within this guide would not be possible without the support of numerous people and organizations. As mentioned in the dedication, my love of the mountains would almost certainly not be existent without my Oma and Opa, Christa and Gunter Hussmann, or my parents Peter and Nancy Hussmann. Thank you to Robert Hanna for graciously endorsing this guide, as well as for your ceaseless efforts to protect our State Parks through Range of Light. Tom Harrison and Tom Harrison Maps are owed my deepest gratitude for permission to reprint their outstanding topographic maps. This book would have taken considerably longer to write, or perhaps never reached completion, without the endless and sincere support and encouragement of Lisa McKinley. I owe many thanks to numerous outdoor gear companies for providing me with demo equipment, including: Easton Mountain Products trekking poles, JetBoil stove, SteriPen water purification, ExOfficio technical apparel, and Sierra Designs sleeping bag. Thank you also to Oboz Footwear and MHM Packs for the most comfortable and durable boots and pack I've had the pleasure of hiking with. The Pacific Crest Trail Association, Tahoe Rim Trail Association, US Forest Service, and numerous other organizations deserve immense gratitude and respect for the beautiful trails they have constructed. Lake of the Sky Outfitters in South Lake Tahoe, CA has been a tremendous resource and point of motivation. Last but not least, thank you to my wonderful trail dog, Bodhi, for still loving me after dragging you on so many questionable hikes with the promise of alpine lakes to swim in.

PREFACE

I was born and raised in South Lake Tahoe, CA. This single fact has shaped my personality and my experiences more than I can put into words. Unfortunately, I did not learn to appreciate this fact until I moved away to attend college in San Luis Obispo, CA. While beautiful in its own right, San Luis Obispo pales in comparison to the cragged peaks, still alpine lakes, lush meadows, and bountiful forests of the Sierra Nevada. While still young on a geologic scale, the Lake Tahoe Basin holds a seemingly timeless and infinite wisdom within its deep glacial valleys. Every feature of the landscape has a unique story to tell, if you take the time to listen.

The relatively young White Fir, Jeffrey Pine, Lodgepole Pine, and numerous other trees tell of a tragic era when the Tahoe basin was almost entirely clear cut for its lumber value, leaving one to imagine what this forest may look like if still populated by the old-growth trees that are now a rarity. The deep U-shaped valleys spread across the south and west shores tell a story of powerful glacial carving that provide the area with its spectacular granitic peaks, valleys, bowls, and cirques. The volcanic rock formations near Carson Pass and on the north shore weave a tale of the fiery and tumultuous eruptions that formed part of the Tahoe basin, ultimately damming its outlet and allowing Lake Tahoe to fill into the spectacular wonder it is today.

Everywhere you travel in this region is remarkable and unique. Microclimates and ecosystems change rapidly with every step taken down the trail, revealing a picture that takes a full lifetime, and maybe more, to truly understand and appreciate. Lake Tahoe is truly a special place. Every inch and every nook and cranny of these mountains offer a sense of wonder and discovery if you allow your eyes to truly open. In the years since moving away from this special place, I have felt my eyes open just a little wider every winter or spring break and every summer.

Perhaps no summer has opened my eyes wider than this past one, when I made the conscious decision to explore these mountains with no other obligations. Purposely unemployed and purposely free, I set out to hike to many places in Tahoe I had never been, and to revisit old favorites with a new eye of appreciation. Five hundred and twenty miles later, I have seen more in my hikes this past summer than I have in the last twenty-four years combined. Yet, not even five hundred plus miles and a summer free of obligation even begins to scratch the surface of everything the Lake Tahoe Basin has to offer. I have seen so much this summer, and still I haven't seen anything at all.

The beauty of these mountains lies in the fact that one could spend a lifetime exploring their bounty, and still not be able to explore it all. The mountains will forever retain a sense of mystery, its features always drawing us into more adventures in hopes of scratching the surface just a little more. The constant allure of discovery and exploration lies within each of us. It is my hope that this guide book helps others discover these mountains in the way I've been able to growing up here. I hope the hikes described in these pages spark in you a sense of deep appreciation for the beauty and mystery these mountains hold. But for now, the mountains are calling, and I must go.

-Aaron M. Hussmann
South Lake Tahoe, CA

INTRODUCTION

"Most people who travel look only at what they are directed to look at. Great is the power of the guidebook maker, however ignorant."
-John Muir

ABOUT THIS BOOK

The words by John Muir above, are the guiding philosophy with which this book is written. This trail guide is not intended as a guide to every inch of trail or every bit of flora and fauna. This guide is not intended to hold your hand as you hike through the wilderness. Rather, the purpose of this guidebook is to give you the best information necessary in reaching your destination, while leaving the all-important sense of discovery in your hands. This book is a valuable resource for describing routes and "need to know" information. However, certain details (i.e. specific campsites, flora/fauna, unimporant terrain details, etc.) have been purposely omitted to allow the reader the opportunity to reveal these details on his/her own. The true beauty in hiking/backpacking, lies in opening your eyes and your senses to the world around you and letting the unknown fill your mind with a sense of wonder and revelation. In that spirit, this guidebook was crafted. I urge you to use this book as a catalyst to your own exploration and discovery.

More than 70 hikes covering over 500 miles of trail are represented in the following pages. In each hike description you will find key mileage markers, elevation information, round trip duration, and the rating of each hike. Following this key information, you will find route descriptions highlighting necessary information and key points. Read these route descriptions carefully and study the maps provided at the start of each chapter. In addition, I strongly recommend the reader purchase their own trail map of the Tahoe area. Tom Harrison Maps (the maps used in this book) offer stunning shaded-relief topographic maps of the area, and this author never hikes without one.

This book should serve as a resource to introduce the reader to a plethora of hikes in the South Lake Tahoe area. In the pages that follow, you will find crucial information regarding rules and regulations, campfire information, leave no trace principles, wildlife, and survival.

USING THIS BOOK

Each hike in this book is highlighted by key distance, elevation, and difficulty details at the top of the description. You will find distances from the trailhead to relevant junctions or geographic locations on the hike. Immediately below these mileages, you are provided with elevation data including net gain or loss. Finally, each hike is given a difficulty rating along with the estimated round trip time for each hike.

To calculate your own round trip time, use this helpful rule of thumb:

(Round Trip Miles) / (2.0 Miles per hour average pace) + (30 minutes for each 1,000 feet of elevation gain)

ex) A 12.0 mile round trip hike with 2,000 feet of elevation gain would take:

12.0 miles / 2.0 miles per hour = 6 Hours
+30 minutes for each 1,000 feet = 1 Hour
= 7 Hours Roundtrip

These times are an estimate only. Your actual hiking time will vary depending on your own pace and external factors. Similarly, any distance information given is as accurate as possible, but in some cases may be inaccurate. Exercise your best judgment when planning a hike.

Each hike description also contains driving information, "Need to Know" bullet points, and alternate routes when possible. Read your hike description carefully, and when necessary refer to other sources of information to aide in your planning.

LAKE TAHOE PERMITS, RULES, AND REGULATIONS

Most of the Lake Tahoe area falls under the jurisdiction of the Lake Tahoe Basin Management Unit of the United States Forest Service. As such, most of these hikes are subject to the rules and regulations set forth by the LTBMU and USFS. Read this information carefully, as violation of these rules and regulations may result in substantial fines, jail, and/or legal action.

Day Use and Overnight Permits

There are five wilderness areas and one roadless area in the Lake Tahoe area supervised by the USFS under different jurisdictions. Most of these areas require a permit year-round for both day use and overnight use.

Desolation Wilderness: Permits are required for day use and overnight use. Permits can be issued by either the Pacific Ranger District or the Lake Tahoe Basin Management Unit.

> -Group size is limited to 12 people per group.
> -Day use permits can also be self-issued at most major trailheads during the summer months.
> -A quota system is in effect for overnight stays in Desolation Wilderness.
> -Overnight users must pay an overnight use fee, and must obtain their permit in person at one of the Forest Service offices listed below.

Meiss Country Roadless Area: Permits are not currently required for day-use or overnight use for any destinations in this area. Fire restrictions may be in effect during summer months. Refer to page 13 for details.

Contact Information:

Pacific Ranger District

Located four miles east of Pollock Pines on Highway 50.
7887 Highway 50, Pollock Pines, CA 95726
Phone: (530) 644-6048 (general information)
(530) 647-5415 (reservations)
Winter: Weekdays only. After April 1st, Monday through Saturday.
Summer: Open Daily, 8:00 a.m. to 4:30 p.m. through October.

Taylor Creek Visitor Center

Located three miles north of the Highway 50/89 junction at South Lake Tahoe, on Highway 89.
Phone: (530) 543-2674
Hours: The Visitor Center will open daily beginning Memorial Day

weekend through the month of October, hours will vary.

Lake Tahoe Basin Management Unit Forest Supervisor's Office
Located two miles east of the Highway 50/89 junction in South Lake Tahoe on Highway 50. From Hwy 50 turn right on Al Tahoe Blvd. and then turn right at first signal.
Address: 35 College Drive, South Lake Tahoe, CA 96150
Phone: (530) 543-2600
Hours: Weekdays from 8:00 a.m. to 4:30 p.m., year-round.

Campfire Permits and Regulations
A valid California Campfire Permit is required to operate any stove, lantern, charcoal barbecue, or wood fire outside of a developed campground. These permits are issued free of charge at any of the forest service offices listed above. Campfire permits are also subject to current fire restrictions and regulations. **CAMPFIRES ARE NEVER ALLOWED IN DESOLATION WILDERNESS.**

During dry summers, fire restrictions often go into effect that prohibit all wood fires, even with a valid California Campfire Permit. In extreme years, stoves, lanterns, barbecues and other similar items have been prohibited as well. Refer to current area fire restrictions by calling any of the above offices, or checking online at http://www.fs.usda.gov/ltbmu

WILDERNESS ETHICS

Lake Tahoe is a beautiful, special place. We are fortunate that countless individuals have dedicated untold effort to preserve and protect the Lake of the Sky. It is up to each of us, as backcountry travelers, hikers, backpackers, and visitors to continue this legacy by practicing these simple tips on any outing.

Plan ahead and prepare:

- Familiarize yourself with the route prior to any outing to reduce unnecessary travel.

- Pack out any trash and food waste you pack in.

Travel and camp on durable surfaces:

- Camp on durable surfaces. These include established trails and campsites, rock, gravel, dry grasses or snow.
- Always camp <u>at least 200 feet</u> from any water source.

Dispose of waste properly:

- Pack it in, pack it out.
- Dig "cat holes" at least 200 feet from water, ensure the hole is at least 6-8 inches deep, and cover/fill the hole thoroughly when done. Pack out all toilet paper in a ziploc bag.
- Wash dishes 200 feet from any water source with biodegradable soap such as Dr. Bronner's or CampSuds.

Take Only Pictures, Leave Only Footprints:

What you find in the wilderness should stay in the wilderness. Refrain from picking plant life, disturbing rocks, pine cones, logs, etc.

Minimize campfire impacts:

- Maintain a small, controllable fire only. Avoid building large bonfires and excessive fire pits.
Remember, NO FIRES IN DESOLATION WILDERNESS.

Respect wildlife:

- View from a safe, respectful distance.
- Never feed wildlife, and always secure food properly (See Page 15 for more details).
- Keep pets from harassing or scaring wildlife.

WILDLIFE INTERACTIONS

Tahoe's wildlife can often be abundant and spectacular. With respectful and responsible tactics, wildlife can be enjoyed free of incident.

Black Bears

Black Bears in Tahoe are often shy of human interaction, and remain focused on food for much of the year. Although bear encounters are rare in proportion to the number of visitors to Tahoe each year, a few simple tips can help make any interactions safe and incident free.

-Never leave food, toiletries, or scented items around camp, in your tent, or in your sleeping bag.
- Store food, toiletries, and scented items in bear proof canisters or lockers. You may also hang your food using proper techniques. See next page for details on storing food.
- If you are lucky enough to encounter a bear, keep a safe respectful distance.
- Never run from a bear.
- Make yourself appear as large as possible.
- If unnoticed by the bear, remain calm and quiet as the bear quietly passes on.
- If necessary, bang pots and pans, blow whistles, and make as much noise as possible to deter the bear.
- Never block a bear's escape route, and never get between a bear and her cubs.

Although attacks are rare (there hasn't been a single reported fatality from a wild black bear in California's history), if you are attacked, fight back aggressively.

A young black bear at Taylor Creek in South Lake Tahoe.

Bear Food Storage Techniques

1) Bear Proof Canisters - Available at most outdoor stores and sometimes for free from the Forest Service, bear canisters provide the ultimate food storage, as well as a stool to sit on in camp. Be sure to properly secure the lid on your canister before storing for the night. Remember to still keep the canister at least 75 yards away from your campsite to keep bears and wildlife out of your camp.

2) Bear Bagging - This involves hanging your food from a sturdy tree branch. The ideal hanging spot will be at least 15 feet off the ground, and 10-15 feet away from the tree trunk. For detailed instructions, see Appendix A on page 142.

Mountain Lions

Mountain Lions are typically found wherever deer are present, and can inhabit a wide array of different environments and terrain.

When hiking in mountain lion territory:
- Never hike alone.
- Do not approach a mountain lion, and never run from a mountain lion to avoid stimulating its instinct to chase.
- Appear as large as possible.
- Fight back aggressively if attacked.

Coyotes

Coyotes are an elusive and often rare sight in the backcountry. They tend to avoid human confrontation. However, if hiking with small dogs or children, keep them under close supervision. Should you encounter a coyote, make as much deterring noise as possible.

PREPARATION

Adequate preparation can make or break a backcountry trip. The Sierra Nevada are notorious for fast-changing weather that can take an afternoon from clear skies and sunshine to thunder and lightning. The terrain and difficulty of a hike may change rapidly. Unfortunately, accidents do happen. Being well prepared can serve as the key difference in survival.

Ten Essentials

The Ten Essentials of hiking and backpacking are items you should absolutely not leave home without. The distance, duration, or difficulty of a hike are irrelevant when considering the ten essentials. **The following items should always be in your pack:**

-Map
-Compass or GPS
-Sunglasses and Sunscreen
-Extra Food
-Extra Water
-Extra Clothing/Insulation
-Headlamp or Flashlight
-First Aid Kit
-Fire Starter
-Knife

In addition, the Ten Essentials can be supplemented by field repair kits, emergency shelter, water purification, signaling devices, and toilet paper/trowel, among others.

Water

Plan your water necessity according to the hike length, availability of water on the hike, and your water purification system. It is recommended that you consume one liter of water for every two hours of hiking, with more water necessary on particularly hot or strenuous hikes. Familiarize yourself with any water sources if you plan to filter water along the hike. Be aware that many water sources can be seasonal and are often dry in the late summer months. When in doubt, always err on the side of carrying more water with you.

Water purification is ALWAYS recommended to avoid harmful viruses and bacteria such as Giardia and Cryptosporidium. Filter water from running water sources as much as possible, avoiding standing or stagnant water except in emergency scenarios. A vast array of portable water purification options exist including tablets, drops, UV lamp filters, pump devices, and in-line filters.

Trail Etiquette

A few simple rules can make your hiking experience and the experience of others more enjoyable. Among some commonly observed practices provided by the American Hiking Society are:

• Hike quietly. Speak in low voices and turn your cell phone down, if not off. Enjoy the sounds of nature and let others do the same.

• If taking a break, move off the trail a ways to allow others to pass by unobstructed.

• Don't toss your trash – not even biodegradable items such as banana peels. If you packed it in, pack it back out.

• Hikers going downhill yield to those hiking uphill. Hikers yield to horses and pack animals, while mountain bikers should yield to hikers.

• When bringing a pet on a hike, be sure to keep it on a leash and under control. Don't forget to pack out pet waste as well.

• Don't feed the wildlife.

• Leave what you find.

• When relieving yourself outdoors, be sure to do so 200 feet away from the trail and any water sources. Follow Leave No Trace principles.

• Walk through the mud or puddle and not around it, unless you can do so without going off the trail. Help preserve the trail by staying on the trail.

• If hiking in a group, don't take up the whole width of the trail; allow others to pass.

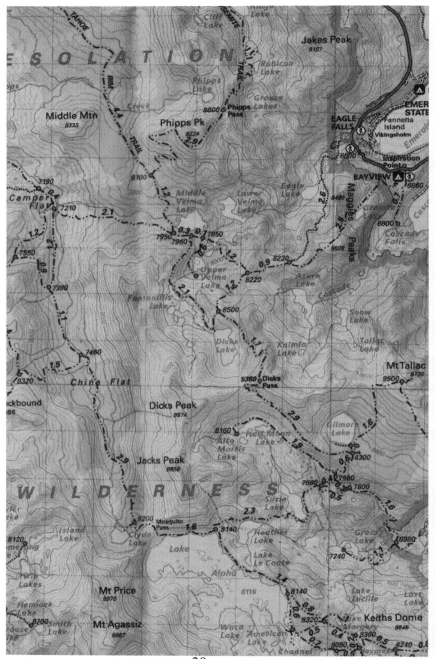

BAYVIEW/EAGLE FALLS TRAILHEAD

DESTINATION	MILES FROM TRAILHEAD	PAGE
Cascade Falls	0.7	22
Eagle Lake	0.9	23
Granite Lake	1.0	24
Maggie's Peaks	1.6+	25
Snow Lake	3.0	26
Azure Lake	3.5	28
Velma Lakes Basin	4.8-5.5*	29
Dick's Lake	5.0	31
Fontanillis Lake	5.7	32
Dick's Peak	7.0	34
Camper Flat	7.3	35

*Denotes multiple routes from this trailhead

Driving:

From South Lake Tahoe, follow Highway 89 north toward Emerald Bay for 8.3 miles from the intersection of Highway 50 and 89. Observe the brown sign indicating the Bayview Trailhead on the left side of the highway across from Inspiration Point. For the Eagle Falls trailhead, continue north on Highway 89 until observing the well-signed Eagle Falls Trailhead on the left side of the Highway. A parking fee is required at the Eagle Falls Trailhead. Both Trailheads are popular destinations, and parking is limited.

CASCADE FALLS
BAYVIEW TRAILHEAD

Destinations	Distance From Start
Cascade Falls	0.7 MI
Round Trip	1.4

Elevation Start: 6,860' End: 6,800' Gain: -60'
Time: 1 to 2 hours   Difficulty: Easy

Best for: Day Hike

Description:

During the height of the late-spring snowmelt, Cascade Falls is one of the most photographed and most visited areas in the Tahoe basin. Begin your hike at the Bayview Trailhead across from Inspiration Point on Highway 89. Immediately from the parking lot you are presented with the option of going to Cascade Falls or to Desolation Wilderness. Bear to the left following the sign for the falls.

The trail climbs slightly over a small ridge that serves as the lateral moraine to the former glacier that carved out Cascade Lake and the preceding valley. After this short climb the trail descends at a mellow rate to the bottom of the U-shaped valley above Cascade Lake. After 0.7 miles you will arrive at the pools just above Cascade Falls. The trail officially ends here with a network of social trails weaving throughout the landscape to different picturesque destinations.

This also serves as the beginning of the trail towards Snow Lake and Azure Lake (Page 26) by following Cascade Creek up the valley to the west. If continuing towards these lakes you will need a free Desolation Wilderness day-use permit from the trailhead. If Cascade Falls is your final destination, no permit is needed.

Driving:

Refer to the Bayview Trailhead driving directions on Page 21

Need to Know:

-No Desolation Wilderness permit is required for Cascade Falls.
-The falls can be fast-flowing and dangerous in the early summer. Use caution when exploring around water's edge.

Eagle Lake seen from the trail to Velma Lakes Basin

EAGLE LAKE
EAGLE FALLS TRAILHEAD

Destinations	Distance From Start
Eagle Lake	0.9 MI
Round Trip	1.8

Elevation Start: 6,600' End: 7,000' Gain: 400'
Time: 1 to 2 hours   Difficulty: Easy

Best for: Day Hike, Overnight

Description:
     Close enough to the trailhead to offer an accessible hike for all, yet far enough to give you the feel of a true "backcountry" lake, Eagle Lake is a perfect introductory hike to the Tahoe area and Desolation Wilderness. Begin your hike from the Eagle Falls Trailhead on Highway 89. Follow the well marked trail to Eagle Falls, gaining slight elevation by way of perfectly constructed rock steps. Cross the bridge spanning Eagle Falls, pausing to snap a few pictures of the roaring cascade during the early summer.
     Continue up the rocky trail, entering Desolation Wilderness a short
23

distance from Eagle Falls. The trail emerges in an open granite slab yielding spectacular views of Emerald Bay. After a short 0.9 mile hike from the trailhead you will find yourself at the shores of this magnificent lake, surrounded by towering granite peaks in a small bowl. A few camping options exist along the shoreline with an overnight permit. Eagle Lake also serves as the entry point for many of the other hikes in the area by continuing uphill at a junction just before Eagle Lake.

Driving:

Refer to the Eagle Falls Trailhead driving directions on Page 21.

Need to Know:

-A free day-use permit available at the trailhead is required if going all the way to Eagle Lake. If Eagle Falls is your only destination, no permit is required.
-For overnight trips, you must obtain an overnight permit in advance (see page 12 for details).

GRANITE LAKE
BAYVIEW TRAILHEAD

Destinations	Distance From Start
Granite Lake	1.0 MI
Round Trip	2.0

Elevation Start: 6,860' End: 7,680' Gain: 820'
Time: 1 to 2 hours   Difficulty: Moderate

Best for: Day Hike, Overnight

Description:

Offering a short but surprisingly steep hike, Granite Lake is tucked in a small forested bowl one thousand feet above Cascade Lake. Your hike begins from the Bayview Trailhead, following signs for Desolation Wilderness rather than Cascade Falls. The trail begins to climb immediately, almost brutally at times. After approximately 15 minutes of climbing, you are offered a view of Emerald Bay worthy of the "Bayview" namesake.

Here the trail bears left and continues climbing up a slightly more mellow drainage up to Granite Lake. Although the hike is only 1.0 mile, the 820 feet

24

of elevation gain in that distance make Granite Lake a rewarding hike. Limited camping options exist due the the steep shoreline surrounding the lake. Hikers seeking a longer trip can continue up the trail toward Maggie's Peaks.

Driving:
> Refer to the Bayview Trailhead driving directions on page 21.

Need to Know:
-For day hikes, please fill out a free day-use permit at the trailhead for entry to Desolation Wilderness.
-For overnight trips, you must obtain an overnight permit in advance (see page 12 for details).

MAGGIE'S PEAKS
BAYVIEW TRAILHEAD

Destinations	Distance From Start
Granite Lake	1.0 MI
Maggie's Saddle	1.3
Maggie's South	1.6
Maggie's North	1.7
Round Trip	3.4+

Elevation Start: 6,860'   End: 8,699'   Gain: 1,839'
Time: 2 to 3 hours . Difficulty: Hard

Best for: Day Hike, Peakbagging

Description:
> Maggie's Peaks offer stunning bird's eye views of Emerald Bay and Cascade Lake, and panoramic views of Lake Tahoe and Desolation Wilderness. Begin this steep hike from the Bayview Trailhead, hiking into Desolation Wilderness toward Granite Lake. This is a steep trail, climbing 820 feet in the first mile, and an additional 1,000 feet to the summit of Maggie's South.

> After a rest at Granite Lake, continue climbing arduously to the low saddle between Maggie's North and Maggie's South. Use caution, as the north side of the saddle can often hold snow and ice well into summer. Once at the saddle, Maggie's South is a relatively straightforward forested approach to the

summit. Bear left at the junction, following a network of social trails that all lead to the summit. After 0.3 miles and approximately 400 feet of gain, you will find yourself in the open summit area of Maggie's South.

Maggie's North can be slightly more difficult, and is not recommended for canine companions. From the saddle, bear right along the initially sandy path that quickly turns into large boulder hopping. Continue to pick your way across the ridge, occasionally requiring Class 3 scrambling to attain the obvious summit.

Driving:

Refer to the Bayview Trailhead driving directions on Page 21.

Need to Know:

-For day hikes, please fill out a free day-use permit at the trailhead for entry to Desolation Wilderness.

-Dogs are not recommended for Maggie's North due to Class 3 bouldering.

Snow Lake
Bayview Trailhead

Destinations	Distance From Start
Cascade Falls	0.7 MI
Snow Lake	3.0
Round Trip	6.0

Elevation Start: 6,860'   End: 7,400'   Gain: 540'
Time: 3 to 4 hours   Difficulty: Moderate
Note: Route Finding May Be Difficult

Best for: Day Hike, Overnight

Description:

An often unknown trail through dense, lush forest and open granite slabs, Snow Lake offers one of the most beautiful hikes in Desolation Wilderness. This route starts from the Bayview Trailhead, taking the trail toward Cascade Falls. A word of caution is in order, however, as route finding past Cascade Falls can become very difficult in places. This may not be the best trip for novice hikers.

From Cascade Falls, follow the path upstream on an old social trail that is no longer maintained. The trail stays in the bottom of the glacial valley, mostly following the stream the entire distance through lush ferns, dense aspen, and beautiful open country. You encounter the first difficulty with route finding when emerging in open granite terrain. Head to the upper left corner of the granite slab, meeting a waterfall. Keep an eye out for rock cairns, but when in doubt, continue to follow near the stream and stay in the bottom of the valley.

After approximately 2.5 miles, begin looking for a fork in the stream to the left, as this is the outlet from Snow Lake. Again the route-finding becomes difficult in this area, so continue to follow the streams when in doubt. After climbing over a small terminal moraine ridge, Snow Lake comes into view with a plethora of open lunch/campsite options. Snow Lake can also be combined with a hike to Azure Lake (page 28) by continuing straight at the fork in the stream, rather than bearing left to Snow Lake.

Driving:
Refer to the Bayview Trailhead driving directions on page 21.

Need to Know:
-For day hikes, please fill out a free day-use permit at the trailhead for entry to Desolation Wilderness.
-For overnight trips, you must obtain an overnight permit in advance (see page 12 for details).

Azure Lake seen from the southern slope

Azure Lake
Bayview Trailhead

Destinations	Distance From Start
Cascade Falls	0.7 MI
Azure Lake	3.5
Round Trip	7.0

Elevation Start: 6,860'   End: 7,720'   Gain: 860'
Time: 3.5 to 5 hours   Difficulty: Moderate
Note: Route Finding May Be Difficult

Best for: Day Hike, Overnight

Description:
     Featuring a cascading waterfall and steep cliffs mirrored in reflective blue waters, Azure Lake is a gem of the Desolation backcountry. From the Bayview Trailhead, follow the same route instructions as the Snow Lake route on the previous page. The key difference in reaching Azure Lake instead of Snow Lake simply lies in continuing to follow the stream straight through the canyon rather than bearing left at the fork to Snow Lake.

From the fork, however, the faint trail climbs a steep 400' in the remaining 0.5 miles. Some sections of Class 3 scrambling may be required, but remember that all uphill routes near the stream will take you to Azure Lake. Once at the lake, spend a fair amount of time exploring the beautiful shoreline. A few limited camping options are available in the less rocky sections of the shoreline. Be sure to bring plenty of insect repellent during the early summer months.

Driving:

Refer to the Bayview Trailhead driving directions on page 21.

Need to Know:

-For day hikes, please fill out a free day-use permit at the trailhead for entry to Desolation Wilderness.

-For overnight trips, you must obtain an overnight permit in advance (see page 12 for details).

Velma Lakes Basin

Destinations	Distance From Start
Bayview Jct.	2.6 MI
Middle Velma Lake	4.8
Upper Velma Lake	5.3
Lower Velma Lake	5.5
Round Trip	9.6+

Elevation Start: 6,600' End: 7,950' Gain: 1,350'
Time: 5 to 8 hours   Difficulty: Hard

Best for: Day Hike, Overnight

Description:

A collection of open, granite-rimmed lakes, Velma Lakes Basin offers a plethora of overnight and dayhiking options in the heart of Desolation Wilderness. Begin your hike from the Eagle Falls or Bayview trailheads, hiking 2.6 miles and 2.8 miles, respectively, until reaching the junction of the two trails. Both trails gain a quick 1,000' of elevation in just over one mile, making for a grueling climb. Very little water is available between the trailhead and Velma Lakes Basin, so be sure to bring plenty for this strenuous portion.

At the intersection of the Bayview and Eagle Falls trails, continue hiking along a relatively flat ridge for 0.9 miles. Here you are presented with the junction to Dick's Lake (page 31). Bear right following signs for The Velmas or Middle Velma Lake. The trail descends through open granite and sparse Whitebark Pine until you reach a lower unnamed lake below Upper Velma Lake. Crossing the stream here may require taking off your boots in the early summer months.

Immediately following the stream crossing, you arrive at the signed junction for Upper Velma Lake. To access Upper Velma Lake, bear left at the junction for 0.6 miles, arriving at the southern shore of Upper Velma Lake resting in the shadows of Dick's Peak. For Middle Velma Lake, continue straight at the previous junction for an additional 0.1 miles before joining with the Pacific Crest Trail. Here the trail parallels Middle Velma Lake approximately 80 feet above the shoreline. Down-climb to access the shore of Middle Velma Lake, or continue on the PCT to explore the rest of the shoreline. Continuing this direction also yields the junction to Camper Flat (page 35) and serves as a route to hike Phipps Peak (refer to map on page 20).

There is no official trail to Lower Velma Lake, but instead a faint social trail leading to this less-traveled lake. At the Upper Velma Junction, a very faint social path bears right (northeast) for approximately 0.7 miles cross-country. When in doubt, hike downhill following the stream you just crossed before the junction, as this is the inlet for Lower Velma Lake. Lower Velma Lake is lined by granite cliffs on most of the shoreline, making camping options considerably more limited. Camping options are plentiful at Upper Velma and Middle Velma Lakes, however.

Driving:

Refer to the Eagle Falls Trailhead driving directions on page 21.

Need to Know:

-For day hikes, please fill out a free day-use permit at the trailhead for entry to Desolation Wilderness.

-For overnight trips, you must obtain an overnight permit in advance (see page 12 for details).

Dick's Lake in the early morning, with Dick's Peak visible (top right).

Dick's Lake

Destinations	Distance From Start
Bayview Jct.	2.6 MI
Dick's Lake Jct.	3.5
Dick's Lake	5.0
Round Trip	10.0

Elevation Start: 6,600' End: 8,420' Gain: 1,820'
Time: 5 to 8 hours   Difficulty: Hard

Best for: Day Hike, Overnight, Peakbagging

Description:

Tucked into the large bowl just beneath Dick's Peak, Dick's Lake offers a fantastic overnight option and breathtakingly reflective waters in the morning. Begin this hike from either the Eagle Falls or Bayview Trailhead, hiking 2.6 and 2.8 miles, respectively, until reaching the junction where the two trails merge. Continue west along the ridge toward Velma Lakes Basin for 0.9 miles until reaching the junction for Dick's Lake.

Bear left at this junction, climbing a mellow 300 feet in 1.2 miles. Along this route you will also encounter a small pond that serves as the headwaters to Upper Velma Lake. This route meets the Pacific Crest Trail on the open ridge just above Dick's Lake. Continue downhill for an additional 0.3 miles until reaching the official junction a few hundred yards from the shore. Continuing on the PCT takes you to Fontanillis Lake.

Descending to Dick's Lake offers impressive views of the north facing bowl on the opposite shore and a plethora of overnight camping options. The lake also serves as a good "base camp" for hiking Dick's Peak (page 34).

Driving:

Refer to the Eagle Falls and Bayview Trailhead driving directions on page 21.

Need to Know:

-For day hikes, please fill out a free day-use permit at the trailhead for entry to Desolation Wilderness.

-For overnight trips, you must obtain an overnight permit in advance (see page 12 for details).

-Please remember there are no fires allowed in Desolation Wilderness.

Fontanillis Lake

Destinations	Distance From Start
Bayview Jct.	2.6 MI
Dick's Lake	5.0
Fontanillis Lake	5.7
Round Trip	11.4

Elevation Start: 6,600'   End: 8,320'   Gain: 1,720'
Time: 6 to 8 hours   Difficulty: Hard

Best for: Day Hike, Overnight

Description:

Fontanillis Lakes may be one of the most picturesque lakes in Desolation Wilderness, yet despite lying directly on the PCT, it is often overlooked in favor of the nearby Velmas and Dick's Lake. This lake can be reached from either the Eagle Falls or Bayview Trailheads. Follow the same route instructions as Dick's Lake on the preceeding page for 5.0 miles.

Rather than descending to the shore of Dick's Lake, bear right and continue on the Pacific Crest Trail for an additional 0.7 miles. Fontanillis Lake becomes visible after 0.5 miles and yields incredible views of Dick's Peak and Dick's Pass. Camping options are somewhat limited here due to the narrow, rocky shoreline. Due to the limited camping, however, you are more likely to find true "desolation" at this lake compared to many others in the wilderness.

Driving:

Refer to the Eagle Falls and Bayview Trailhead driving directions on page 21.

Need to Know:

-For day hikes, please fill out a free day-use permit at the trailhead for entry to Desolation Wilderness.

-For overnight trips, you must obtain an overnight permit in advance (see page 12 for details).

-Please remember there are no fires allowed in Desolation Wilderness.

Reflective Fontanillis Lake with Dick's Pass and Dick's Peak looming.

Dick's Peak

Destinations	Distance From Start
PCT Junction	4.7 MI
Dick's Pass	6.4
Dick's Peak	7.1
Round Trip	14.2

Elevation Start: 6,600'   End: 9,974'   Gain: 3,374'
Time: 7 to 9 hours   Difficulty: Strenuous

Best for: Day Hike, Overnight, Peakbagging

Description:

Standing in the center of Desolation Wilderness, Dick's Peak offers unrivaled 360 degree views from the summit. To obtain the summit from the Eagle Falls or Bayview Trailheads, hike 2.6 or 2.8 miles respectively to the point where the two trails intersect. Continue to proceed westward into Desolation Wilderness, following the trail along the ridge.

After hiking 0.9 miles from the Bayview/Eagle junction, bear left at the junction to Dick's Lake for an additional 1.2 miles before intersecting with the Pacific Crest Trail. Continue to the left, taking the PCT southbound toward Dick's Pass for 1.7 miles of climbing. Once on the open ridge of Dick's Pass, you will see an obvious social trail tackling the ridge to Dick's Peak. The trail fades in and out along the ridge, but all roads lead to the summit.

All told, this route requires several strenuous climbs for a net elevation gain of 3,374 feet. Unlike other routes to Dick's Peak, this option only allows for 0.9 miles of flat hiking, making for a grueling day of constant uphill. Dick's Lake and Fontanillis Lake serve as good base camps if you wish to turn this into an overnight trip.

Driving:

Refer to the Eagle Falls and Bayview Trailhead driving directions on page 21.

Need to Know:

-For day hikes, please fill out a free day-use permit at the trailhead for entry to Desolation Wilderness.

-For overnight trips, you must obtain an overnight permit in advance (see page

12 for details).
-Bring plenty of water and/or a water filter on this grueling hike.

Alternate Routes:
Dick's Peak can also be reached from the Glen Alpine trail and from the summit of Jack's Peak (pages 54-58).

The less-travelled Rockbound Valley seen from Mosquito Pass

Camper Flat

Destinations	Distance From Start
PCT Junction	4.8 MI
Camper Flat Jct.	5.1
Camper Flat	7.3
Round Trip	14.6

Elevation Start: 6,600' End: 7,200' Gain: 600'
Time: 7 to 9 hours   Difficulty: Hard

Best for: Overnight

Description:

Camper Flat lies in the trough of the less-traveled Rockbound Valley running through the heart of Desolation Wilderness, and serves as an access point to many spectacular lakes on the western side of the wilderness. Begin your trip from either the Eagle Falls or Bayview Trailhead and follow the same route instructions for Middle Velma Lake (Page 29). Camper Flat can be considered somewhat of an "up-and-over" hike, as you will gain significant elevation in the beginning just to lose that elevation again in your descent to Camper Flat.

Once reaching the Pacific Crest trail after 4.8 miles, continue along the southern shore of Middle Velma Lake for an additional 0.3 miles. Here you encounter the junction that descends to Camper Flat. Bear left and follow the trail through hemlock forests and glacial erratics for 2.2 miles. Although the trail is well defined along this section, some route finding skills are necessary as the trail disappears in the large granite slabs.

From Middle Velma, you descend 700 feet to the bottom of Rockbound Valley where you encounter the Rubicon River and Camper Flat. From here, lakes including Lake Schmidell, 4-Q Lakes, Lake Lois and more may be accessed by an unmaintained loop trail.

Driving:

Refer to the Eagle Falls and Bayview Trailhead driving directions on page 21.

Need to Know:

-For day hikes, please fill out a free day-use permit at the trailhead for entry to Desolation Wilderness.

-For overnight trips, you must obtain an overnight permit in advance (see page 12 for details).

-Please remember that no campfires are allowed in Desolation Wilderness.

Alternate Routes:

Camper Flat can be accessed by other multi-day trips from the Glen Alpine and Echo Lakes Trailhead (see map on Page 20).

"Wander here a whole summer, if you can. Thousands of God's wild blessings will search you and soak you as if you were a sponge, and the big days will go by un-counted. If you are business-tangled, and so burdened by duty that only weeks can be got out of the heavy-laden year ... give a month at least to this precious reserve. The time will not be taken from the sum of your life. Instead of shortening, it will indefinitely lengthen it and make you truly immortal."

-John Muir

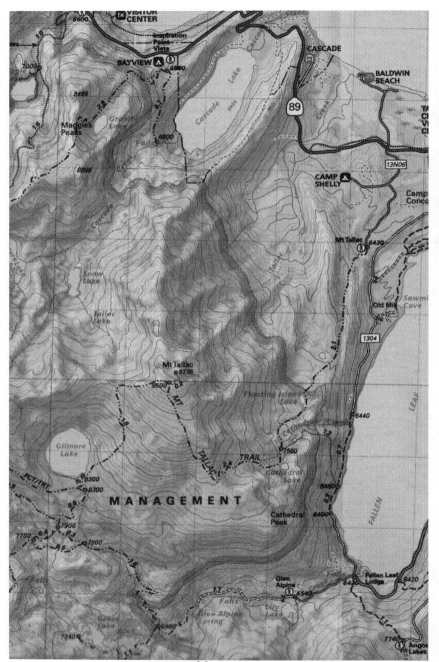

Mt. Tallac Trailhead

Destinations	Distance From Start
Floating Island Lake	1.5 MI
Cathedral Lake	2.1
Mt. Tallac Summit	4.5
Round Trip	9.0

Elevation Start: 6,430'   End: 9,735'   Gain: 3,305'
Time: 4.5 to 8 hours   Difficulty: Strenuous

Best for: Day Hike, Peakbagging

Description:

One of the most popular peaks in the Lake Tahoe basin, and for good reason. Mt. Tallac prominently rises over 3,500 feet from the lake shore. Begin your hike from the Mt. Tallac Trailhead and climb steadily for 2.1 miles to Cathedral Lake, passing Floating Island Lake and yielding your first spectacular views of Lake Tahoe. Cathedral Lake will be the last water before the summit, so make sure to bring plenty with you on this strenuous hike.

The brunt of the climb begins after Cathedral Lake, gaining 2,000' in just 2.4 miles. The trail switchbacks through the southeast facing bowl until you arrive on the summit ridge. Use caution in the late-spring/early-summer months, as large snowfields and cornices may still exist in the bowl. From here the trail continues to climb, although at a much mellower rate for approximately 1.5 miles to the summit. Enjoy plentiful views of Lake Tahoe, Desolation Wilderness, and Carson Pass from the summit before beginning your descent.

Driving:

From South Lake Tahoe, head north on Highway 89 toward Tahoe City for 4 miles from the junction of Hwy 50/89. Following signs for the Mt. Tallac Trailhead, turn left and continue to follow the road for 1 mile to the trailhead parking lot.

Need to Know:

-Please fill out a free day-use permit available at the trailhead. Permits are required for all entry into Desolation Wilderness.
-Bring plenty of water. This is a long, strenuous hike with limited shade.

-Avoid taking dogs. The rocky, talus trail wreaks havoc with their paws. Dogs have been airlifted from the summit at the owner's expense.

Lake Tahoe and Cascade Lake from Mt. Tallac Summit

Alternate Routes:
There are two additional routes to summit Mt. Tallac:

1) A longer, but more mellow approach can be taken up the back side of the mountain via the Glen Alpine Trailhead (see page 51).
2) A slightly shorter but significantly steeper approach can be taken from the south end of Fallen Leaf Lake. This trail is less maintained and less frequented (see next page).

Mt. Tallac Alternate Route

Destinations	Distance From Start
Cathedral Lake	1.7 MI
Mt. Tallac Summit	4.2
Round Trip	8.4

Elevation Start: 6,400' End: 9,735' Gain: 3,335'
Time: 4.5 to 8 hours   Difficulty: Strenuous

Best for: Day Hike, Peakbagging

Description:
 The summit of Mt. Tallac can also be reached by a slightly shorter, but steeper, route from the south end of Fallen Leaf Lake. Starting from Stanford Camp, follow an old social trail northbound as it gains elevation while contouring the lake shore. After 0.3 miles, bear left at a junction, quickly gaining elevation on an unmaintained and ungraded trail. You will gain approximately 1,100 feet of elevation in just 1.7 miles to Cathedral Lake, but will be rewarded with spectacular views of Fallen Leaf Lake. Approximately 1.5 miles from the trailhead, you will join the traditional Mt. Tallac trail. Bear left here and continue towards Cathedral Lake, following the Mt. Tallac directions on the previous pages for the remainder of the hike.

Driving:
 From SLT, head north on Highway 89 toward Tahoe City. Just after Camp Richardson, turn Left on Fallen Leaf Lake Road. Follow this road for 5.5 miles. Turn right at the fire station, following signs for Stanford Camp until the road dead ends.

Need to Know:
 -There are no Desolation Permits at this trailhead. You will need to get a free day-use permit from the Glen Alpine Trailhead (page 43) or from any of the Forest Service locations on pages 12-13.
 -This trail is steep and unmaintained, not recommended for novice hikers.

GLEN ALPINE TRAILHEAD

DESTINATION	MILES FROM TRAILHEAD	PAGE
Angora Peak	2	44
Grass Lake	2.8	45
Susie Lake	4.1	46
Gilmore Lake	4.3	47
Heather Lake	5	48
Half Moon/Alta Morris Lake	5.5	49
Mt. Tallac Summit	4.0/5.9*	51
Clyde Lake	7.7	52
Dick's Peak	7.8+	54
Jack's Peak	7.5/8.5*	55-58

*Denotes multiple routes from this trailhead

Driving:
From SLT, head north on Highway 89 toward Tahoe City. Just after Camp Richardson, turn Left on Fallen Leaf Lake Road. Follow this road for 5.5 miles, passing the main marina and the fire station until arriving at the Glen Alpine Trailhead.

Angora Peak

Destinations	Distance From Start
Angora Ridge	1.1 MI
Angora Peak	2.0
Round Trip	4.0

Elevation Start: 6,400'   End: 8,588'   Gain: 2,188'
Time: 2 to 3 hours   Difficulty: Strenuous

Best For: Day Hike, Peak Bagging

Description:
       Often overlooked, Angora Peak offers exceptional views of Fallen Leaf Lake, Lake Tahoe, and Desolation Wilderness. Start your climb from an unmarked trail lying between the Fallen Leaf Lake firehouse and chapel (not the Glen Alpine trailhead). The trail climbs 700 feet in the first mile, bringing you to Angora Ridge. From here, divert from the trail to the right to climb the ridge leading to Angora Peak.
       Stay to the north side of Angora Peak, as the south and east aspects are littered with boulder fields and cliff bands. All roads lead to the summit on this grueling and unrelenting uphill hike. There may be some Class 2 or 3 scrambling involved as you near the summit. After taking in the view from the top, experienced hikers can traverse the ridge to Indian Rock and Echo Peak via technical Class 3 scrambling. If Angora Peak is the only peak on your list today, avoid the temptation to descend the south face toward Angora Lakes due to aforementioned cliff bands.

Driving:
       See directions for the Glen Alpine Trailhead on page 43, but park near the firehouse instead of continuing to the trailhead.

Alternate Routes:
       Start your hike from the Angora Lakes parking lot and traverse the ridge up the north side of Angora Peak, cutting the mileage in half. However, this parking lot is often full by 9 a.m.

Grass Lake

Destinations	Distance From Start
Glen Alpine Springs	1.1 MI
Gilmore Lake Jct.	1.7
Grass Lake	2.8
Round Trip	5.6

Elevation Start: 6,540' End: 7,240' Gain: 700'
Time: 2 to 3 hours Difficulty: Easy

Best For: Day Hike, Overnighters

Description:

Grass Lake is an easily attainable and rewarding lake set in the trough of the glacial valley that leads to Fallen Leaf Lake. From the Glen Alpine Trailhead, the first mile of the trail takes you down an old dirt/gravel road leading to Glen Alpine Springs, giving you occasional vistas of roaring Glen Alpine Falls. At the springs, the road turns into trail as you begin climbing to the Grass Lake/Gilmore Lake junction at 1.7 miles.

Follow the signpost to Grass Lake for 1.1 miles through forest and riparian environments. In early summer months, crossing the outlet from Grass Lake can be challenging but easily passable by way of a large log across the stream. Once at Grass Lake, take in the spectacular views of Cracked Crag, Jack's Peak, and the outflow waterfall from Susie Lake.

Driving:

See directions to the Glen Alpine Trailhead on page 43.

Need to Know:

-For day hikes, you must fill out a free day-use permit to enter Desolation Wilderness, available at the trailhead.
-For overnight trips, you must obtain an overnight permit in advance (see page 12 for details).

Dick's Peak and the Jack's Peak ridge seen from Susie Lake

Susie Lake

Destinations	Distance From Start
Glen Alpine Springs	1.1 MI
Pacific Crest Trail Jct.	3.8
Susie Lake	4.1
Round Trip	8.2

Elevation Start: 6,540' End: 7,840' Gain: 1,300'
Time: 4 to 6 hours Difficulty: Moderate

Best for: Day Hike, Overnight

Description:
Lying in the heart of Desolation Wilderness surrounded by towering granite peaks, Susie Lake is the epitome of an alpine lake. From the Glen Alpine trailhead, follow an old gravel road for 1.1 miles to Glen Alpine Springs, passing thunderous Glen Alpine Falls on the way. The true climb begins from this point until the junction with the Pacific Crest Trail. This talus covered trail offers spectacular views of the glacial valley responsible for Fallen Leaf Lake.

Continue from the Grass Lake junction for 1.6 miles to the next junction, following the sign for Lake Aloha. At this point you also have the option of hiking 1.0 mile to Gilmore Lake or 2.6 miles to the summit of Mt. Tallac.

Once at the PCT, bear left and continue a short distance to Susie Lake, rewarding yourself with a swim in this alpine lake. Be sure to explore the shoreline before your return hike. Alternatively, you may continue another 0.9 miles to Heather Lake. If camping at Susie Lake, explore the south and west shores of the lake for the best campsites. Also, please remember that there are no fires allowed in Desolation Wilderness.

Driving:
See directions to the Glen Alpine Trailhead on page 43.

Need to Know:
-For day hikes, you must fill out a free day-use permit to enter Desolation Wilderness, available at the trailhead.
-For overnight trips, you must obtain an overnight permit in advance (see page 12 for details).

Gilmore Lake

Destinations	Distance From Start
Pacific Crest Trail Jct.	3.6
Gilmore Lake Jct.	4.2
Gilmore Lake	4.3
Round Trip	8.6

Elevation Start: 6,540' End: 8,380' Gain: 1,840'
Time: 4.5 to 6 hours   Difficulty: Moderate

Best for: Day Hike, Overnight, Peakbagging

Description:
Gilmore Lake is a popular overnight destination and stopping point on the way up to the Mt. Tallac summit. From the Glen Alpine Trailhead, ascend for 3.6 miles to the junction with the Pacific Crest Trail, hiking through rocky terrain with impressive views of the surrounding glacial valley. At the PCT junction, bear right and begin a steady 400' climb over the next 0.7 miles. Be sure to bring plenty of water, as much of the 1,800 feet of elevation gain on this hike are

in direct sun.

Gilmore Lake lies in a bowl of metamorphic rock at the base of Mt. Tallac. The best campsites will be on the southern shore of the lake, as the opposite shore consists of steep talus slopes typically only suitable for marmots. From here, you may continue an additional 1.6 miles while gaining 1,300' to reach Mt. Tallac.

Driving:

See directions to the Glen Alpine Trailhead on page 43.

Need to Know:

-For day hikes, you must fill out a free day-use permit to enter Desolation Wilderness, available at the trailhead.

-For overnight trips, you must obtain an overnight permit in advance (see page 12 for details).

-Please remember that there are no fires allowed in Desolation Wilderness.

Heather Lake

Destinations	Distance From Start
Pacific Crest Trail Jct.	3.8
Susie Lake	4.1
Heather Lake	5.0
Round Trip	10.0

Elevation Start: 6,540'   End: 7,920'   Gain: 1,380'
Time: 5 to 7 hours   Difficulty: Moderate

Best for: Day Hike, Overnight

Description:

With stellar views of the Crystal Range and a true feeling of high alpine hiking, Heather Lake is an incredibly underrated Desolation lake. The approach to this hike follows the same route as Susie Lake (page 46). Continue past Susie Lake for an additional 0.9 miles to the outlet of Heather Lake. This mile of trail is some of the most scenic in Desolation Wilderness. Hiking above the tree line, your views of the surrounding peaks and valleys are unobstructed.

Upon arriving at Heather Lake, the trail follows along the rocky northern shoreline until reaching a grove of hemlocks at the inlet. Most camping for Heather Lake will be on the northern and western shores of the lake, though the rocky terrain makes campsites limited. The inlet of Heather Lake also serves as a main, unmarked route to Jack's Peak (see Page 56).

Driving:

See directions to the Glen Alpine Trailhead on page 43.

Need to Know:

-For day hikes, you must fill out a free day-use permit to enter Desolation Wilderness, available at the trailhead.

-For overnight trips, you must obtain an overnight permit in advance (see page 12 for details).

-Refer to your permit for regulations regarding camping near water. While campsites right on the shore are tempting, they are destructive to the fragile alpine ecosystem and jeopardize future recreation in the area.

Alternate Routes:

Heather Lake can also be reached via the Echo Lakes Trailhead (map on page 60). The total distance is approximately 7.5 miles one-way, or 5 miles one-way if you elect to take the water taxi, bypassing Echo Lakes.

Half Moon/Alta Morris Lakes

Destinations	Distance From Start
Pacific Crest Trail Jct.	3.6 MI.
Half-Moon Lake	5.5
Round Trip	11.0

Elevation Start: 6,540' End: 8,160' Gain: 1,620'
Time: 5.5 to 8 hours   Difficulty: Moderate

Best for: Day Hike, Overnight, Peakbagging

Description:

Often bypassed in favor of the more popular Gilmore Lake and Mt. Tallac Summit, Half Moon and Alta Morris Lakes are hidden gems tucked in a massive bowl underneath towering Dick's and Jack's Peaks. Begin your hike from the Glen Alpine Trailhead, following signs for Gilmore Lake and Mt. Tallac. You will pass the junction for Grass Lake (1.7 mi), and at the next junction (3.3 mi) follow signs for Gilmore Lake. Continue a short 0.3 miles to the junction with the Pacific Crest Trail.

Crossing the PCT, follow signs for Half Moon Lake for an additional 1.9 miles of trail weaving through glacial moraines and seasonal tarns. You will actually arrive at the eastern edge of Half Moon Lake after approximately 1.0 mile. Continue following a social trail through thick grass along the northern shore of Half Moon Lake. The trail ends on the western shore, at a point allowing you to see Alta Morris Lake and Half Moon Lake simultaneously. Dick's Peak and Jack's Peak loom impressively over this basin, with a magnificent waterfall draining from two tarns into Half Moon Lake. Camping options are limited due to the rocky terrain, but the best sites are located in between the two lakes. As an overnight trip, these lakes act as a perfect base camp to bag Dick's and Jack's Peak (see pages 54-58).

Driving:
See directions to the Glen Alpine Trailhead on page 43.

Need to Know:
-For day hikes, you must fill out a free day-use permit to enter Desolation Wilderness, available at the trailhead.
-For overnight trips, you must obtain an overnight permit in advance (see page 12 for details).
-In the early summer months be sure to bring mosquito repellent.

Half Moon and Alta Morris Lakes with Jack's Peak

Mt. Tallac Summit

Destinations	Distance From Start
Pacific Crest Trail Jct.	3.6 MI.
Gilmore Lake	4.3
Mt. Tallac Summit	5.9
Round Trip	11.8

Elevation Start: 6,540'   End: 9,735'   Gain: 3,195'
Time: 6 to 9 hours   Difficulty: Strenuous

Best for: Day Hike, Peakbagging

Description:
      An iconic peak in the Lake Tahoe basin, the Mt. Tallac summit often sees upwards of 100 visitors per day in the summer months. The route from the Glen Alpine Trailhead takes a considerably longer approach that also makes the climb less difficult than the main route on the front side. Follow the trail to Gilmore Lake (Page 47) for 4.3 miles. You will gain approximately 1,800' in these first miles, followed by an additional 1,300' in just 1.6 miles to the summit of Mt. Tallac. This elevation gain makes Gilmore Lake a perfect rest stop before the final summit push.

      From Gilmore Lake, the trail bears right and begins to climb the eastern slope of the lake. Emerging above the treeline, the trail continues to climb to the rocky summit. Enjoy breathtaking views of Lake Tahoe and Desolation Wilderness from the summit before beginning your descent back to Gilmore Lake.

Driving:
      See directions to the Glen Alpine Trailhead on page 43.

Need to Know:
-Please fill out a free day-use permit for Desolation Wilderness, available at the Trailhead.
-For overnight trips, you must obtain an overnight permit in advance (see page 12 for details).
-Bring plenty of water. This is a long, strenuous hike with limited shade.
-Avoid taking dogs. The rocky, talus trail wreaks havoc with their paws. Dogs have been airlifted from the summit at the owner's expense.

Alternate Routes:
There are two additional routes to summit Mt. Tallac:
1) The more popular front side trail is 3 miles shorter but significantly steeper. (Page 39).
2) An even shorter and steeper approach can be taken from the south end of Fallen Leaf Lake. This trail is less maintained and less frequented (see map on page 41).

Clyde Lake from the West Shore. Mosquito Pass visible as the low notch in the top-left portion of the photo.

Clyde Lake

Destinations	Distance From Start
Pacific Crest Trail Jct.	3.8 MI.
Lake Aloha	6.1
Clyde Lake	7.7
Round Trip	15.4

Elevation Start: 6,540' End: 8,080' Gain: 1,540'
Time: 7 to 10 hours   Difficulty: Hard

Best for: Day Hike, Overnight

Description:

A true hidden gem, Clyde Lake lies in a deep glacial cirque below Mt. Price at the head of Rockbound Valley. Begin your hike from the Glen Alpine Trailhead, following signs for Gilmore Lake/Lake Aloha for 3.8 miles until you intersect with the Pacific Crest Trail. Wind your way through beautiful high country past Susie Lake and Heather Lake for an additional 2.3 miles until you reach Lake Aloha.

From here you will bear right, away from the PCT and toward Mosquito Pass. The term "pass" seems to be used loosely here as the hike requires just a short uphill before descending to Clyde Lake for an additional 1.6 miles from the Lake Aloha junction. Camping options are few and far between here, but well worth the search. Clyde Lake rests in the shadow of Mt. Price and Jack's Peak, fed by a seasonal waterfall on the southwest slope. For the ambitious hiker, you can venture a Class 3 scramble through talus and boulders to reach the base of the falls. An overnight trip is preferable to a day hike to truly enjoy this hidden treasure.

Driving:

See directions to the Glen Alpine Trailhead on page 43.

Need to Know:

-For day hikes, you must fill out a free day-use permit to enter Desolation Wilderness, available at the trailhead.

-For overnight trips, you must obtain an overnight permit in advance (see page 12 for details).

-Refer to your permit for regulations regarding camping near water. While campsites right on the shore are tempting, they are destructive to the fragile alpine ecosystem and jeopardize future recreation in the area.

Alternate Routes:

Clyde Lake can also be reached via Echo Lakes Trailhead (see page 78). One-way distance on this route is 9.0 miles, or 6.5 miles if you elect to take the water taxi and bypass Echo Lakes.

Dick's Peak

Destinations	Distance From Start
Pacific Crest Trail Jct.	3.6 MI.
Dick's Pass	7.1
Dick's Peak	7.8+
Round Trip	15.6+

Elevation Start: 6,540' End: 9,974' Gain: 3,434'
Time: 8 to 12 hours   Difficulty: Strenuous

Best for: Day Hike, Overnight, Peak Bagging

Description:

  Anchored in the center of Desolation Wilderness, Dick's Peak offers spectacular views of Desolation that other peaks do not afford. Don't expect Dick's Peak to give up the views easily, however, as the peak either requires an overnight trip or incredibly long day hike. Starting from the Glen Alpine trailhead, follow the trail to Gilmore Lake for 4.2 miles. Rather than going to Gilmore Lake, however, bear left on the Pacific Crest Trail to Dick's Pass for another 2.9 miles of long, sun-exposed climbing.

  Enjoy a break at Dick's Pass before following a faint social trail ascending the ridge to Dick's Peak. The trail here often disappears into the talus that requires Class 3 scrambling. All routes lead to the 9,974 foot summit, but be aware of lingering snow on the north side of the ridge in the early summer. On the summit, take in spectacular views of Lake Tahoe, Dick's and Fontanillis Lakes, Rockbound Valley, the Crystal Range and more. From the summit, you can also traverse the ridge to the south to Jack's Peak via technical Class 3 scrambling (see next entry). For overnight trips, suitable base camps can be established at Half Moon Lake (Page 49), Gilmore Lake (Page 47), and Dick's Lake (Page 31).

Driving:

  See directions to the Glen Alpine Trailhead on page 43

Need to Know:

-For day hikes, you must fill out a free day-use permit to enter Desolation Wilderness, available at the trailhead.

-For overnight trips, you must obtain an overnight permit in advance (see page 12 for details).

-Bring plenty of water, or a water filter, if attempting Dick's Peak as a day hike.

Alternate Routes:

Dick's Peak can also be reached from the Eagle Falls or Bayview Trailheads (page 34) for a slightly shorter day hike. The summit can also be reached via Jack's Peak, essentially reversing the Dick's to Jack's route.

Jack's Peak Via Dick's Peak

Destinations	Distance From Start
Pacific Crest Trail Jct.	3.6 MI.
Dick's Peak	7.8+
Jack's Peak	8.5+
Round Trip	17.0+

Elevation Start: 6,540' End: 9,856' Gain: 3,316'
Time: 9 to 12 hours Difficulty: Strenuous

Best for: Day Hike, Overnight, Peak Bagging

Description:

Jack's Peak offers impressive views of Rockbound Valley, Desolation Wilderness, and peaks as far south as Carson Pass. For the ambitious and skilled hiker, Jack's Peak can be attained in combination with a day summiting Dick's Peak. Follow the same route described in the Dick's Peak hike on the previous page (or see an alternate route for Dick's peak on Page 34).

From the summit of Dick's Peak, head due south on the ridge toward the obvious summit of Jack's Peak. You will quickly lose 500 feet of elevation, only to gain back 400 feet to reach the summit. Attaining Jack's Peak requires technical Class 3 climbing on a route that holds snow into the early summer months. After enjoying the fruits of your labor on the summit, you can either reverse your route back to Dick's Peak, or descend the drainage to the southeast down to Heather Lake and the Pacific Crest Trail (recommended). Take it slow and easy on the descent, as you will quickly lose 1,800' through steep, rocky terrain.

Driving:

See directions to the Glen Alpine Trailhead on page 43.

Need to Know:

-For day hikes, you must fill out a free day-use permit to enter Desolation Wilderness, available at the trailhead.

-For overnight trips, you must obtain an overnight permit in advance (see page 12 for details).

-Bring plenty of water, or a water filter, if attempting Dick's and Jack's Peak as a day hike.

Alternate Routes:

See the next entry for the route up the Heather Lake drainage to the summit of Jack's Peak.

Jack's Peak Via Heather Lake

Destinations	Distance From Start
Pacific Crest Trail Jct.	3.8 MI.
Heather Lake	5.0
Jack's Peak	7.5+
Round Trip	15.0+

Elevation Start: 6,540' End: 9,856' Gain: 3,316'
Time: 6 to 9 hours Difficulty: Strenuous

Best for: Day Hike, Overnight, Peakbagging

Description:

Jack's Peak is more easily attained by following the drainage from the inlet of Heather Lake to Jack's southeast bowl (route highlighted on next page). From the Glen Alpine Trailhead, follow the same route to Heather Lake as described on Page 48 for 5.0 miles. Find the inlet stream (sometimes seasonal) to Heather Lake on the northwest shore in a grove of hemlocks. As the trail begins to switchback, divert from the path and begin to follow the drainage for a steep 1,800' climb. After approximately 1.5-2 miles of climbing, the drainage ends in a large open bowl covered by talus. Make your way to the low point in the ridge to the north.

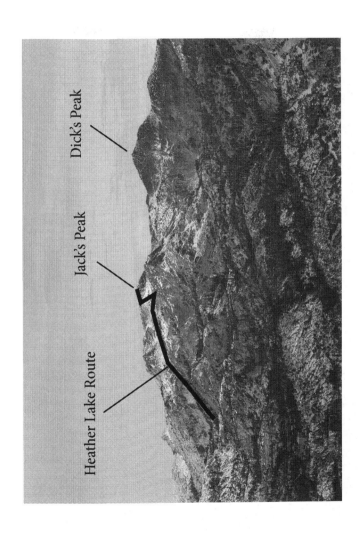

Once you reach this ridge you will be able to see Dick's Peak. From here, bear left up the ridge and discover a network of social trails that lead to Jack's Peak for the final summit push. Enjoy spectacular views of Lake Aloha, Clyde Lake, the Crystal Range, Rockbound Valley, and Dick's Peak from the summit. You can continue on to Dick's Peak by descending the Class 3 ridge, or reverse your route for the descent back to Heather Lake.

Driving:
See directions to the Glen Alpine Trailhead on page 43.

Need to Know:
-For day hikes, you must fill out a free day-use permit to enter Desolation Wilderness, available at the trailhead.
-For overnight trips, you must obtain an overnight permit in advance (see page 12 for details).
-Bring plenty of water, or a water filter, if attempting Dick's and Jack's Peak as a day hike.

*"At last the lake burst upon us...
a noble sheet of blue water lifted
six thousand three hundred feet
above the level of sea, and walled
in by snow-clad mountain peaks
that towered aloft full three thousand feet higher still... I thought it
must surely be the fairest picture
the whole earth affords."*

-Mark Twain

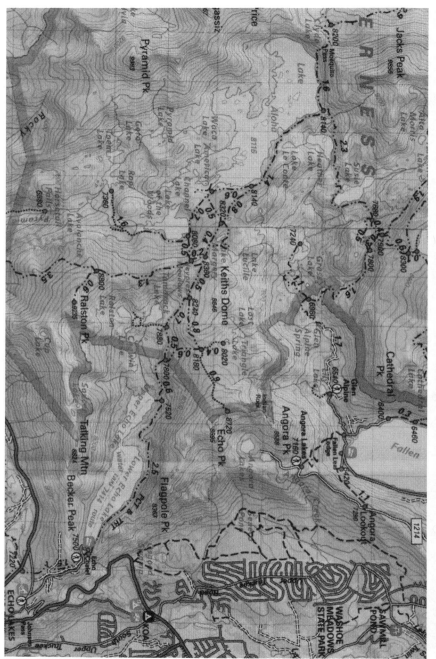

60

ECHO LAKES TRAILHEAD

Note: You may take a water taxi across Echo Lakes, in which case, subtract 2.5 miles from many of these destinations.

DESTINATION	MILES FROM TRAILHEAD	PAGE
Becker Peak	1	62
Flagpole Peak	1.3	63
Talking Mountain	1.7	64
Upper Echo Lake	2.5	65
Tamarack, Ralston, Cagwin Lakes	4.0+	66
Ralston Peak	4.0/6.9*	67-70
Triangle Lake	4.1	71
Echo Peak	5	72
Lake of the Woods	5.5	74
Lake Lucille	5.6	75
Lake Aloha	6.0	77
Clyde Lake	9.0	78

*Denotes multiple routes from this trailhead

Driving: From South Lake Tahoe, head west on Highway 50 toward Sacramento. As you head over Echo Summit, a short passing lane emerges with a single lane road branching off to the right. Bear right on this single lane road, then take your second right following signs for Echo Lakes.

Becker Peak

Destinations	Distance From Start
Becker Peak	1.0 MI.
Round Trip	2.0

Elevation Start: 7,500'   End: 8,720'   Gain: 1,220'
Time: 1 to 2 hours   Difficulty: Moderate

Best for: Day Hike, Peakbagging

Description:

Often unmentioned and overlooked, Becker Peak provides surprisingly great views of the Echo Lakes basin, as well as the Carson Pass area to the south. Begin this short hike from the Echo Lakes Chalet parking area. Head southbound on the Pacific Crest/Tahoe Rim Trail for only 0.1 mile. Upon reaching the first switchback of the climb, the PCT will turn left, while your path will take you straight on an old social trail.

As you climb through steep forested terrain, you will pass the rusted remains of a 1950's era pickup truck. Ascend to the ridge and the trail takes you to the south side of Becker Peak where you will make the final push to the summit. The last few feet of the peak require Class 3 scrambling to reach the summit proper. From here, you can continue traversing the ridge to Talking Mountain (Page 64) and Ralston Peak (Pages 67-70), or descend back to Echo Lakes to wrap up this quick day hike.

Driving:

Refer to the Echo Lakes Trailhead directions on page 61.

Need to Know:

-No permits are required if your only destination is Becker Peak. If you continue to Ralston Peak, you will need a Desolation day-use permit.

Flagpole Peak

Destinations	Distance From Start
Flagpole Peak	1.3 MI.
Round Trip	2.6

Elevation Start: 7,500'   End: 8,363'   Gain: 863'
Time: 1 to 2 hours   Difficulty: Moderate

Best for: Day Hike, Peakbagging

Description:

     Standing prominently above the town of Meyers, Flagpole Peak is an impressive granite monolith that offers everything from Class 3 to Class 5 climbs. This hike begins from the Echo Lakes Trailhead and heads north on the Pacific Crest Trail for approximately 0.7 miles. Flagpole Peak comes into view, at which point you may bear right, away from the trail, and start your ascent of the ridge that leads to the summit.

     The next 0.6 miles of your hike will take you cross-country through glacial erratics and across large granite slabs. Below the summit, Class 3 climbing begins for the final push. The summit is marked by a large flagpole with numerous flags and articles of clothing attached. Enjoy the spectacular views of Lake Tahoe and the Echo Lakes basin.

Driving:

     Refer to the Echo Lakes Trailhead directions on page 61.

Talking Mountain

Destinations	Distance From Start
Becker Peak	1.0 MI.
Talking Mtn.	1.7
Round Trip	3.4

Elevation Start: 7,500' End: 8,824' Gain: 1,324'
Time: 1.5 to 2.5 hours Difficulty: Moderate

Best for: Day Hike, Peakbagging

Description:

When viewed from Echo Lakes, Talking Mountain offers a resounding north facing bowl rising dramatically from the lake shore. The summit can be reached as part of a traverse of the south rim of Echo Lakes basin. Traversing west from the summit of Becker Peak, continue on the ridge for an additional 0.7 miles to reach the summit while gaining an additional 100 feet of elevation.

When possible, stay just to the north side of the ridge, as the south side tends to be filled with thick manzanita and snowbrush making bushwhacking difficult. From the summit, you can continue your traverse an additional 2.3 miles to the summit of Ralston Peak, or reverse course back to your starting point at Echo Chalet.

Driving:

Refer to the Echo Lakes Trailhead directions on page 61.

Need to Know:

-Talking Mountain represents the Desolation Wilderness boundary. Please fill out a free day-use permit available at the trailhead.
-The trail disappears frequently on this ridge traverse. Familiarize yourself with the route and bring a map and navigational tools,

Alternate Routes:

The summit of Talking Mountain can also be reached by doing an eastward traverse of the same ridge, starting from Ralston Peak and heading toward Becker Peak.

Upper Echo Lake

Destinations	Distance From Start
Upper Echo Lake	2.5 MI.
Round Trip	5.0

Elevation Start: 7,500' End: 7,520' Gain: 20'
Time: 1.5 to 2.5 hours Difficulty: Easy

Best for: Day Hike

Description:
      Echo Lakes sit spectacularly in a large glacial basin and act as the key to the southern end of Desolation Wilderness. From Echo Lake Chalet, cross the dam of Lower Echo Lake and hike north on the Pacific Crest Trail/Tahoe Rim Trail. The route flanks the northern edge of Echo Lakes, weaving through open glacial erratics, lush forest, and small cabins.

      Alternatively, the Echo Lakes Marina runs a boat taxi during the summer months for $12.00 per person. This taxi bypasses the 2.5 miles section flanking Echo Lakes and drops you off just 0.6 miles from the boundary of Desolation Wilderness. However, it is not uncommon for speedy hikers to out-hike the taxi from end to end. Upon reaching the end of Upper Echo Lake, myriad options become available, the closest being Tamarack, Ralston, and Cagwin Lakes (Page 66).

Driving:
      Refer to the Echo Lakes Trailhead directions on page 61.

Need to Know:
- Sometimes referred to as the "Lake Aloha Freeway," this trail can become quite busy during the summer. Plan an early start to avoid the crowds.
- Please fill out a free day-use permit at the trailhead for entry to Desolation Wilderness.
- For water taxi information, call the Echo Lakes Chalet at 530-659-7207 or visit **www.echochalet.com.**

Tamarack Lake and Ralston Peak

Tamarack, Ralston, and Cagwin Lakes

Destinations	Distance From Start
Upper Echo Lake	2.5 MI.
Tamarack Lake Jct.	3.6
Tamarack Lake	4.0
Round Trip	8.0 +

Elevation Start: 7,500' End: 7,800' Gain: 300'
Time: 4 to 6 hours   Difficulty: Moderate

Best for: Day Hike, Overnight

Description:

Nestled below the towering summit of Ralston Peak, this collection of lakes are the first you will encounter in Desolation Wilderness after entering from the Echo Lakes Trailhead. If bypassing the water taxi, follow the PCT for 2.5 miles around Echo Lakes. From the end of Upper Echo Lake, the trail begins to climb slightly, crossing the wilderness boundary 0.6 miles later. Be sure to take a look over your shoulder and marvel at the impressive Echo Lakes glacial basin.

At the entrance to Desolation Wilderness, you also have the option of bearing right to Triangle Lake (page 71), which additionally serves as the access point to Echo Peak (page 72). For this hike, continue 0.5 miles further into Desolation before coming to the Tamarack Lake junction. From here the trail descends approximately 80 feet to Tamarack Lake. Skirting the eastern edge of the lake, the trail continues in a loop to Ralston Lake and Cagwin Lake which lie just on the other side of a small ridge at the base of Ralston Peak. These lakes offer a plethora of camping options, serving as a perfect trip for beginner backpackers and seasoned veterans alike.

Driving:
Refer to the Echo Lakes Trailhead directions on page 61.

Need to Know:
-For day hikes, please fill out a free day-use permit at the trailhead for entry to Desolation Wilderness.
-For overnight trips, you must obtain an overnight permit in advance (see page 12 for details).
-Please remember there are no fires allowed in Desolation Wilderness.

Ralston Peak Via South Rim Traverse

Destinations	Distance From Start
Talking Mountain	1.7 MI.
Ralston Peak	4.0
Round Trip	8.0 +

Elevation Start: 7,500'   End: 9,235'   Gain: 1,735'
Time: 4 to 6 hours   Difficulty: Hard

Best for: Day Hike, Peakbagging

Description:
Often underappreciated in the shadow of neighboring Pyramid Peak, Ralston Peak offers breathtaking views of Lake Aloha, the Crystal Range, Lake Tahoe, Carson Pass, and the American River Valley. The summit can be reached

by combining this hike with a traverse of the Echo Lakes Basin south rim (see Becker Peak and Talking Mountain on pages 62 and 64). In this case, continue your traverse westward from Talking Mountain. Make your way to the next prominent high point, an unnamed peak slightly higher than Talking Mountain. From here you'll have your first look down into Saucer Lake, perched high above Echo Lakes. It is possible to descend the ridge to this lake, but limited camping is available.

Continuing along the ridge, Class 3 scrambling becomes necessary as you emerge from the hemlocks and climb above the treeline onto a knife edge ridge. Cup Lake, perched on the southern side of the ridge will come into view on your left. Here it may be necessary to down-climb 20-30 feet to your left to safely continue on the ridge. Once around this corner, the terrain opens up and becomes a quick, easy ramp to the summit of Ralston Peak at 9,235'.

From the summit, you can reverse your route on the ridge to return to Echo Chalet, or follow the trail to the southwest to descend down to Haypress Meadows and the Pacific Crest Trail, returning to Echo Lakes along the PCT.

Driving:
Refer to the Echo Lakes Trailhead directions on page 61.

Need to Know:
-Because this ridge traverse has no trail and requires Class 3 scrambling, bring plenty of water and give yourself longer than a normal hike of this distance might take.
-For day hikes, please fill out a free day-use permit at the trailhead for entry to Desolation Wilderness.

Alternate Routes:
Ralston Peak can also be obtained from a steep 4.1 mile trail climbing out of Camp Sacramento on Highway 50 (next page). A much longer but mellower route can be taken by following the PCT from Echo Lakes to Haypress Meadows and bearing left on a trail to Ralston Peak (page 70).

Ralston Peak Via Camp Sacramento Trailhead

Destinations	Distance From Start
Ralston Ridge Jct.	3.5 MI.
Ralston Peak	4.1
Round Trip	8.2

Elevation Start: 6,520'   End: 9,235'   Gain: 2,715'
Time: 4 to 6 hours   Difficulty: Strenuous

Best for: Day Hike, Peakbagging

Description:

    A shorter, yet steeper ascent of this under appreciated peak yields fantastic and rewarding 360 degree views from the summit. Begin this route from the "Mt. Ralston" Trailhead across Highway 50 from Camp Sacramento. This trail rises sharply through White Fir forests and lush riparian environments. As the trail ascends, you begin to rise above the tree line, yielding views of Lover's Leap and the American River Valley.

    In 3.5 miles you will top out on the left flank of the ridge leading to Ralston Peak. If you were to continue straight, the trail would descend down to the PCT, another ascent option for Ralston (page 70). Instead, bear right and follow the trail and occasional rock cairns to the summit.

Driving:

    From South Lake Tahoe, head west on Hwy. 50 toward Sacramento. 2.7 miles after the Sierra-at-Tahoe turn, the pullout for the trailhead will be on your right, across from Camp Sacramento.

Need to Know:

-For day hikes, please fill out a free day-use permit at the trailhead for entry to Desolation Wilderness.
-There is little to no water along this route; bring plenty.

Alternate Routes:

    Ralston Peak can also be reached by a 4.0 mile ridge traverse from Echo Chalet (previous page), or a 6.9 mile ascent following the PCT (next page).

Ralston Peak Via PCT

Destinations	Distance From Start
Lake of the Woods Jct.	4.8 MI.
Ralston Ridge Jct.	6.3
Ralston Peak	6.9
Round Trip	13.8

Elevation Start: 7,500' End: 9,235' Gain: 1,735'
Time: 6 to 8 hours   Difficulty: Strenuous

Best for: Day Hike, Peakbagging, Overnight

Description:

A much longer and more mellow ascent of Ralston Peak suitable for overnight trips can be accomplished via the Pacific Crest Trail. Begin your hike from Echo Chalet, hiking 3.1 miles to enter Desolation Wilderness (the water taxi is also an option to subtract 2.5 miles). Begin climbing an additional 1.7 miles to Haypress Meadows, which serves as a major junction point for trails in the area.

Bear left on the trail following signs to Lake of the Woods. Keep an eye out, however, as you will be turning at another junction in less than 0.2 miles. Rather than continuing to Lake of the Woods, follow the trail south toward Ralston Peak/Hwy 50. The trail climbs through dense forest for 1.3 miles, passing a small meadow and pond formerly inhabited by a goat herder in the early 1900's. At the ridge, bear left toward the summit of Ralston Peak for an additional 0.6 miles. Because of the length of this route, suitable overnight destinations include Lake of the Woods, Lake Margery, or Tamarack Lake.

Driving:

Refer to the Echo Lakes Trailhead directions on page 61.

Need to Know:

-For day hikes, please fill out a free day-use permit at the trailhead for entry to Desolation Wilderness.

-For overnight trips, you must obtain an overnight permit in advance (see page 12 for details).

-Please remember there are no fires allowed in Desolation Wilderness.

Triangle Lake

Destinations	Distance From Start
Triangle Lake Jct.	3.1 MI.
Triangle Lake	4.1
Round Trip	8.2

Elevation Start: 7,500'   End: 8,020'   Gain: 520'
Time: 4 to 5 hours   Difficulty: Moderate

Best for: Day Hike, Peakbagging, Overnight

Description:

One the of smaller named lakes in Desolation Wilderness, Triangle Lake sits above the Glen Alpine valley with sweeping views from Dick's Peak to Tahoe. Access Triangle Lake by beginning from the Echo Lakes Trailhead and heading northbound on the Pacific Crest Trail for 3.1 miles to the Triangle Lake junction and boundary for Desolation Wilderness.

Bear right at the junction, following the trail as it climbs through forest and open country for 0.6 miles, gaining 300 feet in elevation. Arriving at another junction, continue straight following signs for Triangle Lake for an additional 0.4 miles. Alternatively, a right at this junction takes you to the summit of Echo Peak (page 72), while a left returns you back to the Pacific Crest Trail near Haypress Meadows.

Triangle Lake offers a few limited campsites due to its rocky shoreline on one edge, and soggy meadow shoreline on the other. It is also possible to traverse cross-country to the west, maintaining the same elevation as much as possible for approximately 0.5 miles to aptly named Lost Lake. Ambitious hikers may also wish to ascend Keiths Dome (elev. 8,646') by following the ridge cross-country to the west of Triangle Lake.

Driving:

Refer to the Echo Lakes Trailhead directions on page 61.

Need to Know:

-For day hikes, please fill out a free day-use permit at the trailhead for entry to Desolation Wilderness.

-For overnight trips, you must obtain an overnight permit in advance (see page 12 for details).

Mt. Tallac, Angora Peak, Fallen Leaf Lake, and Tahoe from Echo Peak

Echo Peak

Destinations	Distance From Start
Triangle Lake Jct.	3.1 MI.
Echo Peak Jct.	3.7
Echo Peak	5.0
Round Trip	10.0

Elevation Start: 7,500' End: 8,895' Gain: 1,395'
Time: 5 to 6 hours   Difficulty: Moderate

Best for: Day Hike, Peakbagging, Overnight

Description:
Seen prominently from South Lake Tahoe, Echo Peak and its ridge line seem to erupt straight up from the valley below. The easiest line of ascent begins from the Echo Lakes Trailhead and continues north on the PCT for 3.1 miles to

the Triangle Lake junction. Bear right at the junction and climb an additional 0.6 miles to a second junction. Again, bear right at this junction rather than continuing straight to Triangle Lake. A distinct trail continues toward the summit for another 0.9 miles before beginning to disappear at the top of the ridgeline to the left of Echo Peak. The route is easy from here, however, as you simply need to traverse the ridge to the right until the summit comes into view.

From the top, enjoy spectacular rock formations shaped by years of wind, rain, and snowmelt, as well as tremendous views of Desolation Wilderness, Lake Tahoe, and Angora Lakes. This peak is easy enough to accomplish as a day hike, but if you are so inclined, nearby Triangle Lake makes a perfect option for overnight camping.

Driving:
Refer to the Echo Lakes Trailhead directions on page 61.

Need to Know:
-For day hikes, please fill out a free day-use permit at the trailhead for entry to Desolation Wilderness.
-For overnight trips, you must obtain an overnight permit in advance (see page 12 for details).

Alternate Routes:
Echo Peak can be reached through two alternate routes that both involve Class 3 climbing. The first option traverses the ridge from Echo Chalet and Flagpole Peak (page 63) requiring down-climbing to avoid rock buttresses on the ridge. The second option traverses from the north ridge by way of Angora Peak (page 44) and Indian Rock. This section involves hazardous and technical Class 3 climbing with high consequence and should not be attempted by novice hikers.

Lake of the Woods

Destinations	Distance From Start
Desolation Wilderness	3.1 MI.
Lake of the Woods Jct.	4.8
Lake of the Woods	5.5
Round Trip	11.0

Elevation Start: 7,500' End: 8,080' Gain: 580'
Time: 6 to 7 hours   Difficulty: Moderate

Best for: Day Hike, Overnight

Description:

Yielding absolutely spectacular views of Pyramid Peak and Mt. Agassiz, Lake of the Woods is a popular overnight destination for good reason. From the Echo Lakes Trailhead, start your hike north on the Pacific Crest Trail, passing Lower and Upper Echo Lakes and climbing to Haypress Meadows for 4.8 miles. This is a rocky, talus covered trail so be sure to wear sturdy shoes for this hike.

Reaching Haypress Meadows, you will encounter the junction to Lake of the Woods. Bear left at the junction making your way up a small ridge for 0.2 miles, at the top of which you will encounter a second junction. Continue following the signs for Lake of the Woods at this junction. Alternatively, you may also climb the summit of Ralston Peak by bearing left here (page 70).

Making your way to Lake of the Woods, you will begin to descend through Hemlock forests and open slopes of mule's ear, paintbrush, and sage. Take in the spectacular views from the shore and, if camping, find a spot in one of the official designated campsites scattered around the lake.

Driving:

Refer to the Echo Lakes Trailhead directions on page 61.

Need to Know:

-Camping at Lake of the Woods is allowed in designated campsites only. Please obey this requirement to protect endangered species that inhabit the lake shore.
-For day hikes, please fill out a free day-use permit at the trailhead for entry to Desolation Wilderness.
-For overnight trips, you must obtain an overnight permit in advance (see page

12 for details).

Alternate Routes:

Lake of the Woods can also be reached by hiking in from the "Mount Ralston" trailhead on Highway 50 across from Camp Sacramento (see page 69 for details). This route is slightly shorter at 5.3 miles one-way, but is significantly steeper and more strenuous.

Pyramid Peak seen from Lake of the Woods

Lake Lucille

Destinations	Distance From Start
Lake Lucille Jct.	5.2 MI.
Lake Lucille	5.6
Round Trip	11.2

Elevation Start: 7,500' End: 8,200' Gain: 700'
Time: 5.5 to 6.5 hours Difficulty: Moderate

Best for: Day Hike, Overnight

Description:

A pleasant, forested lake situated above the Glen Alpine valley, Lake

75

Lucille offers enjoyable day-hikes and overnight trips alike. Best accessed from the Echo Lakes Trailhead, hike north along the Pacific Crest Trail toward Lake Aloha. You will encounter a myriad of trail junctions in your 5.2 mile hike to the Lake Lucille junction. In order, you will encounter Triangle Lake Jct. (3.1), Tamarack Lake (3.6), Triangle Lake again (4.3), Lake of the Woods (4.8), and finally the Lake Lucille junction at 5.2 miles.

Bear right at the trail junction, descending through forest of hemlock. The trail initially travels along the northern shore of Lake Margery before crossing the Margery outlet/Lucille inlet, bringing you to the southwest shore of Lake Lucille approximately 0.4 miles from the PCT.

Should you find yourself with an abundance of time and a will to explore, consider ascending 8,646' Keiths Dome rising directly from the eastern shore of Lake Lucille. Alternatively, traverse cross-country to the northwest along the obvious ridge, encountering Jabu Lake en route to the 8,872' summit of Cracked Crag.

Driving:
Refer to the Echo Lakes Trailhead directions on page 61.

Need to Know:
-For day hikes, please fill out a free day-use permit at the trailhead for entry to Desolation Wilderness.
-For overnight trips, you must obtain an overnight permit in advance (see page 12 for details).

Alternate Routes:
Lake Lucille might also be obtained from the "Mt. Ralston" trailhead across from Camp Sacramento (page 69) for a hike similar in distance but much more strenuous in elevation gain.

Lake Aloha

Destinations	Distance From Start
Desolation Wilderness	3.1 MI.
Lake Aloha	6.0
Round Trip	12.0

Elevation Start: 7,500' End: 8,116' Gain: 616'
Time: 6 to 7 hours   Difficulty: Moderate

Best for: Day Hike, Overnight, Peakbagging

Description:

Quite possibly one of the most popular destinations for day hikers and overnight backpackers, Lake Aloha's iridescent blue waters lie in stark contrast to the sheer granite walls of Pyramid Peak, Mt. Agassiz, and Mt. Price. This simple and straightforward hike departs from the Echo Lakes Trailhead, heading northbound on the Pacific Crest Trail.

Continue to hike on the PCT and follow all signs for Lake Aloha for 6.0

The Crystal Range rises prominently from Lake Aloha.

miles before arriving at the southeastern shore of the largest lake in Desolation Wilderness. Because of its size, the options for exploration here are boundless. The PCT continues for an additional 1.4 miles along the eastern edge of Lake Aloha, yielding spectacular views that seem to change with every step.

While camping options may seem unlimited, Desolation Wilderness is regulated by a quota system for overnight stays. Due to Lake Aloha's popularity, be sure to reserve your overnight stay in advance. Lake Aloha unlocks myriad opportunities for exploring other lakes and peaks, and serves as a perfect first stop on a multi-day trip through Desolation Wilderness. Lake Aloha is also worth exploring in the late summer, as low water levels can turn it into a series of smaller lakes.

Driving:
    Refer to the Echo Lakes Trailhead directions on page 61.

Need to Know:
-For day hikes, please fill out a free day-use permit at the trailhead for entry to Desolation Wilderness.
-For overnight trips, you must obtain an overnight permit in advance (see page 12 for details).

Alternate Routes:
    Lake Aloha can also be reached from the Glen Alpine Trailhead (page 53) with a one-way hike of 6.1 miles. Additionally, a 6.2 mile hike from the "Mount Ralston" Trailhead at Camp Sacramento (page 69) offers a path to Lake Aloha by connecting with the PCT in Haypress Meadows.

Clyde Lake

Destinations	Distance From Start
Lake Aloha	6.0 MI.
Mosquito Pass Jct.	7.4
Clyde Lake	9.0
Round Trip	18.0

Elevation Start: 7,500'   End: 8,200'   Gain: 700'

Time: 9 to 11 hours   Difficulty: Hard

Best for: Day Hike, Overnight

Description:

Lying just to the north of Mosquito Pass from Lake Aloha, Clyde Lake sits beneath an impressive glacial cirque at the head of Rockbound Valley. To reach this alpine lake from the Echo lakes Trailhead, hike north on the PCT towards Lake Aloha for 6.0 miles. Upon reaching Lake Aloha, continue northbound around the eastern shore of Aloha for 1.4 miles, enjoying breathtaking views of the Crystal Range.

At the northeastern corner of Lake Aloha you will encounter a junction to either continue on the PCT or to branch off to Mosquito Pass. Opt for Mosquito Pass, bearing left on Lake Aloha's north shore. Traveling through a lakeside marsh environment, you contour around the lake for approximately 1 mile before beginning your climb over the pass.

Ascending through forests of hemlock, Mosquito Pass can hardly be considered a pass from this direction, as you only gain approximately 200 feet of elevation before beginning your descent to Clyde Lake. As you climb, however, be sure to look over your shoulder for impressive views of Lake Aloha. Clyde Lake offers limited camping along its northern shore. While sites along the water may be tempting, please respect your permit regulations in order to protect future recreation in this area.

Driving:

Refer to the Echo Lakes Trailhead directions on page 61.

Need to Know:

-For day hikes, please fill out a free day-use permit at the trailhead for entry to Desolation Wilderness.

-For overnight trips, you must obtain an overnight permit in advance (see page 12 for details).

Alternate Routes:

Clyde Lake can also be reached from the Glen Alpine trailhead by hiking 7.7 miles one-way (page 52).

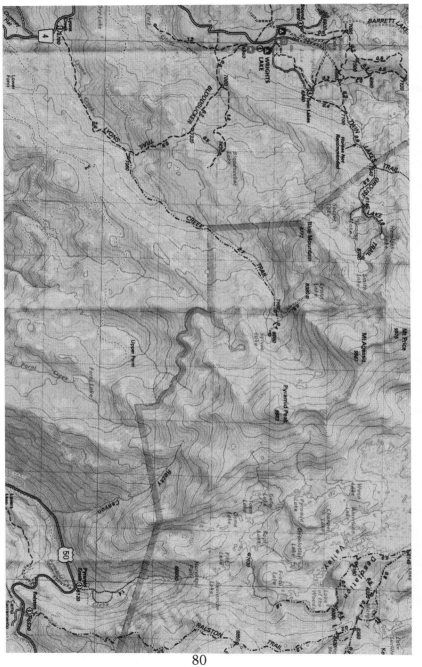

80

DESOLATION WILDERNESS WEST

DESTINATION	MILES FROM TRAILHEAD	PAGE
Lyons Creek Trailhead		
Lake Sylvia	4.6	82
Lyons Lake	4.7	83
Pyramid Peak	5.8	84
Wright's Lake/Twin Lakes Trailhead		
Grouse Lake	2.1	85
Hemlock Lake	2.5	87
Smith Lake	3.1	88
Sayles Canyon/Bryan Meadow		
Bryan Meadow	4.3	91
Sayles Canyon	5.0	92
Other		
Horsetail Falls	1.4	93
Pyramid Peak	3.2	94

*Denotes multiple routes from this trailhead

Driving

From South Lake Tahoe drive west on Highway 50 toward Sacramento for 20 miles. Turn right on Wright's Lake Road. For the Lyon's Creek Trailhead, continue 4.2 miles on Wright's Lake Road before encountering the trailhead on your right. For the Twin Lakes Trailhead, continue on Wright's Lake Road for 8.1 miles, then turn right toward the Twin Lakes Trailhead for an additional 0.9 miles.

Lake Sylvia

Destinations	Distance From Start
Bloodsucker Lake Jct.	1.5 MI
Lake Sylvia	4.6
Round Trip	9.2

Elevation Start: 6,700'   End: 8,060'   Net Gain: 1,360'
Time: 4.5 to 6 hours   Difficulty: Moderate

Best for: Day Hike, Overnight, Peakbagging

Description:

Cupped below the imposing ridge line leading to Pyramid Peak and surrounded by old growth hemlocks, Lake Sylvia is a gorgeous and incredibly accessible lake on the western boundary of Desolation Wilderness. Begin your hike from the Lyons Creek Trailhead off Wrights Lake Road. Hike eastbound through sparse forest contouring Lyons Creek for 1.5 miles before arriving at the side trail to Bloodsucker Lake.

Continue straight at this junction, following the sign for Lake Sylvia. The trail continues to wind through shaded forest before entering Desolation Wilderness, beginning to climb through open granite slabs. The trail crosses Lyons Creek just prior to the junction of Lyons Lake and Lake Sylvia, 4.2 miles in to the hike.

Bear right at the junction, for an additional 0.4 miles before arriving at the western shore of Lake Sylvia. Lake Sylvia offers a variety of camping options along its shores, but please respect any campsite closures or restoration areas.

Driving:

Refer to the Lyons Creek Trailhead driving directions on page 81.

Need to Know:

-Permits are required for all entry into Desolation Wilderness. Obtain a free day use permit at the trailhead, or refer to page 12 for instructions on obtaining an overnight permit.

Lyons Lake

Destinations	Distance From Start
Bloodsucker Lake Jct.	1.5 MI
Lyons Lake	4.7
Round Trip	9.5

Elevation Start: 6,700' End: 8,380' Net Gain: 1,680'
Time: 4.5 to 7 hours Difficulty: Moderate

Best for: Day Hike, Overnight, Peakbagging

Description:

Lyons Lake sits perched on the western flank of the large glacial drainage of Mt. Price and Mt. Agassiz. Begin this moderate hike from the Lyons Creek Trailhead, following the same instructions for Lake Sylvia on the previous page. Continue past the Bloodsucker Lake junction at 1.5 miles, entering Desolation Wilderness and reaching the Lyons Lake junction at 4.2 miles.

Bear left at the junction and begin a steep climb up to Lyons Lake, gaining 400 feet in only 0.5 miles. Lyons Lake lies in open granite at 8,360 feet. From here, it may be possible to summit Mt. Price and Mt. Agassiz by climbing the eastern ridge to Agassiz then traversing to Mt. Price via Class 3 scrambling.

Driving:

Refer to the Lyons Creek Trailhead driving directions on page 81.

Need to Know:

-Permits are required for all entry into Desolation Wilderness. Obtain a free day use permit at the trailhead, or refer to page 12 for instructions on obtaining an overnight permit.

Pyramid Peak

Destinations	Distance From Start
Lake Sylvia	4.6 MI
Pyramid Ridge	5.0
Pyramid Peak	5.8
Round Trip	11.6

Elevation Start: 6,700' End: 9,983' Net Gain: 3,283'
Time: 6 to 9 hours   Difficulty: Strenuous

Best for: Day Hike, Overnight, Peakbagging

Description:

   A centerpiece of Desolation Wilderness, Pyramid Peak is an impressive summit visible from vantage points far across the Tahoe basin. Begin this strenuous hike from the Lyons Creek Trailhead, following the same route instructions for Lake Sylvia on page 82. On this 4.6 mile hike through the valley to Lake Sylvia, you are rewarded with your first views of Pyramid as it crests above the ridge line.

   From Lake Sylvia, follow the path across the lake outlet to the steeper, southern shore of the lake. You are looking to follow a route that leads to an obvious low notch in the ridge line. This involves Class 3 scrambling and climbing through loose rock and scree, but offers the shortest and most accessible ascent of the ridge.

   From the top of the notch, a social trail marked by rock cairns emerges to the left as it climbs up the open ridge toward the summit. Continue following this trail for approximately 0.8 miles, gaining an additional 1,300 feet in the process. All roads uphill lead to the summit, but be sure to take your time and step carefully as you cross the boulder fields leading to the top. From the summit, enjoy spectacular birds-eye views of Lake Aloha and Desolation Wilderness.

Driving:

   Refer to the Lyons Creek Trailhead driving directions on page 81.

Need to Know:

-Permits are required for all entry into Desolation Wilderness. Obtain a free day use permit at the trailhead, or refer to page 12 for instructions on obtaining an overnight permit.

-Familiarize yourself with the map and the route before any off-trail hiking.

Alternate Routes:
The summit of Pyramid Peak can also be reached from a route called Rocky Canyon off Highway 50 (page 94).

A lightly, snow-covered Grouse Lake from the northern shoreline.

Grouse Lake

Destinations	Distance From Start
Twin Lakes Jct.	1.3 MI
Grouse Lake	2.1
Round Trip	4.2

Elevation Start: 6,960' End: 8,140' Net Gain: 1,180'
Time: 2 to 3 hours   Difficulty: Easy

Best for: Day Hike, Overnight

Description:
Lying in a beautiful, partially-forested granite bowl on the western slope of Desolation Wilderness, Grouse Lake offers a pleasant day-hike or over-

night trip for beginner backpackers. Begin your hike from the Twin Lakes Trailhead at Wrights Lake, following signs for Twin Lakes that take you northeastward away from the lake. Follow this trail for 0.4 miles through meadow and forest before reaching your first junction. Bear right at this junction, continuing to follow signs for Twin Lakes.

The trail climbs 400 feet over the next 0.9 miles weaving through forest and open granite slabs. Keep your eyes peeled for rock cairns marking the route through these granite areas. Shortly after entering Desolation Wilderness, you will arrive at the junction to Twin Lakes/Grouse Lake. Bear right at this junction, heading uphill into the open granite. This section of the trail climbs steeply, switchbacking over 0.8 miles to gain an additional 600 feet of elevation, yielding views of Wright's Lake and the valley to the west.

After 2.1 miles of hiking and nearly 1,200 feet of elevation gain from the trailhead, you will arrive at the northern shore of Grouse Lake. Steep rocky terrain lines the opposite shore, while the near shore features marshy and forested terrain. Explore the area to find several marked campsites designated by the Forest Service. These sites are available on a first come, first serve basis.

Driving:
Refer to the Twin Lakes Trailhead driving directions on page 81.

Need to Know:
-Permits are required for all entry into Desolation Wilderness. Obtain a free day use permit at the trailhead, or refer to page 12 for instructions on obtaining an overnight permit.

Hemlock Lake

Destinations	Distance From Start
Twin Lakes Jct.	1.3 MI
Grouse Lake	2.1
Hemlock Lake	2.5
Round Trip	5.0

Elevation Start: 6,960' End: 8,400' Net Gain: 1,440'
Time: 2.5 to 4 hours   Difficulty: Moderate

Best for: Day Hike, Overnight

Description:

A small alpine lake fed by snow melt of the granite bowl surrounding it, Hemlock Lake offers the sense of a remote backcountry experience only a short distance from the trailhead. Begin your hike from the Twin Lakes Trailhead at Wrights Lake, following trail signs for Twin Lakes. Follow the same directions as Grouse Lake on the previous page for the first 2.1 miles. In this stretch, bear right at the first junction at 0.4 miles, then bear right again at the second junction at 1.3 miles toward Grouse Lake.

After the first 2.1 miles and 1,200 feet of elevation gain, you will arrive at Grouse Lake. Continue to follow the trail on the north side of the lake as it skirts the shoreline, then begins to climb the ridge. The route follows the ridge eastward while gaining an additional 300 feet of elevation over the remaining 0.4 miles.

A total of 2.5 miles of hiking brings you to the edge of Hemlock Lake, with a wide, boulder filled bowl serving as the backdrop. Camping at Hemlock Lake is restricted to designated campsites only within 500 yards of the lake. If designated spots are full, you must camp outside this 500 yard radius. From Hemlock Lake, an unmaintained trail marked by rock cairns continues up the basin to Smith Lake (page 88).

Driving:

Refer to the Twin Lakes Trailhead driving directions on page 81.

Need to Know:

-Permits are required for all entry into Desolation Wilderness. Obtain a free day use permit at the trailhead, or refer to page 12 for instructions on obtaining an overnight permit.

Smith Lake seen from the ridge above.

Smith Lake

Destinations	Distance From Start
Twin Lakes Jct.	1.3 MI
Grouse Lake	2.1
Hemlock Lake	3.1
Round Trip	6.2

Elevation Start: 6,960'   End: 8,700'   Net Gain: 1,740'
Time: 3 to 5 hours   Difficulty: Moderate

Best for: Day Hike, Overnight

Description:
    Continuing on from Grouse Lake and Hemlock Lake, Smith Lake

stands at the head of a glacial valley as the largest in this chain of three lakes. Perched beneath an inspiring boulder-filled cirque, Smith Lake is well worth the extra mile. Beginning from the Twin Lakes Trailhead at Wrights Lake, follow the same route instructions to Grouse Lake and Hemlock Lake on the previous pages. A hike of 2.5 miles and 1,400 feet of elevation gain brings you to Hemlock Lake and the end of the maintained trail.

Although the trail past Hemlock Lake is unmaintained, it receives enough use to be relatively well-defined. Continue following this path to the southeast as is climbs 300 feet through hemlock forest, eventually emerging into open granite just prior to reaching Smith Lake. At certain points during this 0.5 mile section, it may be necessary to follow rock cairns to maintain the proper route.

Upon reaching the ridge above Smith Lake, it becomes necessary to scramble downhill to reach the shoreline. Much of the shoreline is steep and rocky here, making camping sites few and far between. For an added challenge, one might wish to ascend an unnamed 9,620' peak above Smith Lake via technical Class 3 scrambling up a large boulder field to gain the ridge to the east. Once on the ridge, bear north and continue to scramble to the summit.

Driving:
Refer to the Twin Lakes Trailhead driving directions on page 81.

Need to Know:
-Permits are required for all entry into Desolation Wilderness. Obtain a free day use permit at the trailhead, or refer to page 12 for instructions on obtaining an overnight permit.

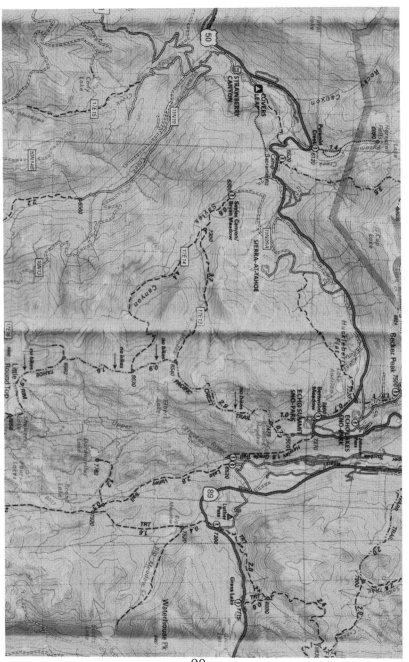

Bryan Meadow

Destinations	Distance From Start
Sayles Canyon Jct.	0.6 MI
Bryan Meadow	4.3
Round Trip	8.6

Elevation Start: 6,800' End: 8,540' Net Gain: 1,740'
Time: 4.5 to 6 hours Difficulty: Moderate

Best for: Day Hike

Description:

Possibly one of the most underrated and overlooked hikes in the South Lake Tahoe area, the Bryan Meadow/Sayles Canyon area offers wonderful exploration of the Pacific Crest and its offshoot canyons. Begin your hike from the Bryan Meadow/Sayles Canyon Trailhead, located behind Sierra-at-Tahoe ski resort. The trail begins to climb up the canyon immediately, gaining 500 feet of elevation through 0.6 miles of old growth Red Fir and Western White Pine.

In a marshy area 0.6 miles from the trailhead, you will arrive at the junction that branches either to Bryan Meadow to the left or up Sayles Canyon to the right. Bear left at this junction, continuing to gain elevation into a small canyon. Shortly, you will find yourself at the base of Sierra-at-Tahoe's backside chairlift, dubbed "The Alley." The trail bears right, away from the ski resort as it makes its way up to the Pacific Crest Trail and Bryan Meadow.

After hiking 3.7 miles from the Sayles Canyon junction and gaining an additional 1,200 feet of elevation, you will find yourself at Bryan Meadow, and the junction with the Pacific Crest Trail. Though no spectacular sweeping views are given, Bryan Meadow offers a plethora of wildflowers and lush alpine meadow life. From this junction, you may either reverse course back to the trailhead, or bear right on the PCT for 0.9 miles before meeting the Sayles Canyon trail and descending through the canyon back to the trailhead.

Driving:

From South Lake Tahoe, drive west on Highway 50 toward Sacramento for 9.8 miles, then turn left on Sierra-at-Tahoe Road. Continue for 1.5 miles before bearing right on a gravel road marked by a green gate. Follow the dirt/gravel road for an additional 2.0 miles through Sierra-at-Tahoe's West Bowl before arriving at the trailhead.

Need to Know:
-This trail is often unused and unmaintained. Familiarize yourself with the route before attempting.

Alternate Routes:
Bryan Meadow can also be reached from the Echo Summit SnoPark trailhead by hiking southbound on the Pacific Crest Trail for 3.9 miles (refer to map on page 90 for details).

Sayles Canyon

Destinations	Distance From Start
Sayles Canyon Jct.	0.6 MI
Bryan Meadow	5.0
Round Trip	10.0

Elevation Start: 6,800' End: 8,630' Net Gain: 1,830'
Time: 5 to 6 hours   Difficulty: Moderate

Best for: Day Hike

Description:
Similar to the Bryan Meadow route, Sayles Canyon is a hidden gem within the Tahoe area, offering a beautiful hike through a glacially carved valley. Begin your hike from the Sayles Canyon/Bryan Meadow Trailhead on the opposite side of the mountain from Sierra-at-Tahoe resort. The trail climbs an initial 500 feet of elevation in the first 0.6 miles before reaching the Bryan Meadow/Sayles Canyon junction. To explore Sayles Canyon, bear right at this junction, crossing a seasonal stream through marshy terrain.

The trail continues to contour a seasonal creek for the majority of the hike, until reaching the headwall of the canyon. Here, the route bears left, following a more conservative route up the canyon wall by avoiding cliff areas that exist on the opposite wall. This last segment gains a steep 640 feet before finally intersecting with the Pacific Crest Trail at 8,630'. From this junction, it is quite enjoyable to complete a 10.2 mile loop of Sayles Canyon and Bryan Meadow. Bear left at the PCT for 0.9 miles before encountering the Bryan Meadow junction, where you will descend back to the trailhead for 4.3 miles.

Driving:

Refer to the Bryan Meadow/Sayles Canyon Trailhead driving directions on page 91.

Need to Know:

-This trail is often unused and unmaintained. Familiarize yourself with the route before attempting.

Horsetail Falls

Destinations	Distance From Start
Horsetail Falls	1.4 MI
Round Trip	2.8

Elevation Start: 6,120'   End: 6,880'   Net Gain: 760'
Time: 1.5 to 3 hours   Difficulty: Hard

Best for: Day Hike

Description:

A popular, breathtaking hike alongside one of the most prominent waterfalls in the Lake Tahoe area, the Horsetail Falls hike is certainly worthwhile. Begin your hike from the Pyramid Creek Trailhead on Highway 50, making sure to pay the $5.00 parking fee. From the parking lot, a well-defined path begins to climb alongside thunderous Pyramid Creek. Continue following this route for the duration of the 1.4 mile maintained trail as it gains 760 feet of elevation.

The trail ends at a spectacular vista with the roaring falls immediately off-trail. It may be possible for the adventurous hiker to continue scrambling alongside Pyramid Creek to reach the Avalanche Lake outlet. However, perform this scrambling at your own caution a safe distance from the falls, this is a treacherous route.

Driving:

From South Lake Tahoe, follow US Highway 50 west toward Sacramento for 13.7 miles. The Pyramid Creek Trailhead is well-signed on the right side of the highway, shortly after a sweeping turn.

Need to Know:

-Keep children and pets away from the edge of the falls. Horsetail falls are incredibly steep and fast-moving. Any fall into the water will result in serious injury and/or death.

Pyramid Peak via Rocky Canyon

Destinations	Distance From Start
Pyramid Peak Summit	3.2 MI
Round Trip	6.4

Elevation Start: 5,920' End: 9,983' Net Gain: 4,063'
Time: 5 to 8 hours   Difficulty: Strenuous

Best for: Day Hike, Peakbagging

Description:

One of the most prominent peaks in the Lake Tahoe area, Pyramid Peak offers stunning 360 degree views of Desolation Wilderness, Carson Pass and the American River Valley. Begin this grueling and relentless uphill hike from an unmarked trail on the side of Highway 50 (see driving info). This route predominantly follows the creek bed responsible for gouging out Rocky Canyon up to the final summit ridge. Not for the faint of heart, this trail climbs approximately 4,000 feet in just 3.2 miles.

As you begin to reach the summit ridgeline, the terrain opens up and begins to mellow out slightly compared to the canyon itself. The trail begins to fade, but continue following it to the best of your abilities while traversing the ridge northbound to the summit. The final approach to the summit takes you through a large boulder field. Use caution as you pick your way through this area, as some boulders may dislodge, causing serious injury. Once on the summit, enjoy the spectacular bird's eye view of Lake Aloha and the surrounding mountains before embarking on your descent.

Driving:

From South Lake Tahoe, drive west on US Highway 50 for 14.4 miles. On the left side of the Highway, just past the Pyramid Creek Trailhead, a small turnout acts as the unofficial trailhead. This turnout is 0.9 miles before the town of Strawberry on Highway 50.

Need to Know:
-This is a steep, strenuous climb. Bring plenty of food and water.

-Because this is not an official trailhead, you must obtain your permit for entry into Desolation Wilderness from another trailhead or from a ranger station. See page 12 for details.

Alternate Routes:

Pyramid Peak can also be reached from the west by following a route through Lake Sylvia for 5.8 miles (see page 84).

Lake Aloha from the summit of Pyramid Peak

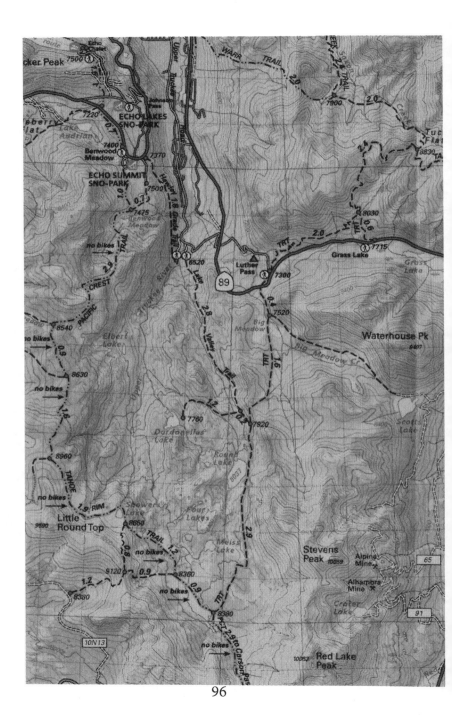

BIG MEADOW AND CARSON PASS

DESTINATION	MILES FROM TRAILHEAD	PAGE
Big Meadow Trailhead		
Scott's Lake	2.4	98
Round Lake	2.5	99
Dardanelles Lake	3.4	100
Waterhouse Peak	4.0*	101
Stevens Peak	4.7*	103
Meiss Meadow	4.9	104
Showers Lake	7.0	105
Carson Pass Trailhead		
Red Lake Peak	2.6	107
Meiss Meadow	2.9	108
Stevens Peak	4.0*	110
Showers Lake	5.0	111

*Denotes alternate and possibly shorter routes.

Driving- Big Meadow:
From South Lake Tahoe, take Highway 50 west toward Sacramento. In the town of Meyers, turn left on Highway 89, travelling south for 5.3 miles. Turn left into the Big Meadow Trailhead.

Driving- Carson Pass
From South Lake Tahoe, take Highway 50 west toward Sacramento. In the town of Meyers, turn left on Highway 89, travelling south for 11.1 miles. Turn right on Highway 88 and continue for 7.3 miles, passing the Carson Pass Ranger station, and parking in the lot on the right side of the Highway.

Scott's Lake

Destinations	Distance From Start
Big Meadow Jct.	0.4 MI
Scott's Lake	2.4
Round Trip	4.8

Elevation Start: 7,300' End: 8,000' Gain: 700'
Time: 2.5 to 4 hours Difficulty: Easy

Best for: Day Hike, Overnight

Description:

Scott's Lake offers an easy day hike for all abilities through dense forest, lush Aspen groves, and open meadows around the base of Waterhouse Peak. Begin your hike from the Big Meadow Trailhead, following signs for Round Lake and Big Meadow. The trail crosses Highway 89 almost immediately and begins to climb approximately 200 feet in elevation before reaching the junction to Scott's Lake.

Bear left at the junction, skirting along the edge of Big Meadow. Alternatively, continuing straight at the junction takes you to Round Lake and Dardanelles Lake, among others (Pages 99-100). The trail continues to climb at a mellow rate, gaining only 500 feet over the next 2.0 miles. Just prior to Scott's Lake you will need to open and re-latch a cattle gate that also marks the boundary of the Lake Tahoe Basin Management Unit. Enjoy a lunch stop at the lake before returning, or find a good campsite along the shoreline for an easy overnight trip.

Driving:

Refer to the Big Meadow Trailhead driving directions on page 97.

Alternate Routes:

Scott's Lake is also accessible by four-wheel drive vehicle from the Hope Valley area on Highway 88 (see map on page 96).

Round Lake

Destinations	Distance From Start
Big Meadow Jct.	0.4 MI
Dardanelles Jct.	2.0
Round Lake	2.5
Round Trip	5.0

Elevation Start: 7,300'   End: 8,037'   Gain: 737'
Time: 2.5 to 4 hours   Difficulty: Moderate

Best for: Day Hike, Overnight

Description:

   With looming volcanic cliffs rising straight from the shoreline, Round Lake offers beautiful scenery and stark contrast to the red cliffs above its waters. Beginning from the Big Meadow Trailhead, hike 0.4 miles across Highway 89, reaching the Round Lake/Scott's Lake junction. Continue straight through the junction into Big Meadow, taking in views of the 10,059' Stevens Peak in the distance.

   From Big Meadow, the trail begins to climb up and over the glacial ridge line separating Round Lake and the Meiss Meadow area from Big Meadow. On the other side of the ridge, the trail descends to the valley floor, meeting with the Lake Valley Trail and bringing you to the junction to Dardanelles Lake. Bear left at this junction to continue on toward Round Lake.

   From this point, the trail continues an additional 0.5 miles, slowly climbing through intriguing volcanic formations before reaching the northern shoreline of Round Lake. A plethora of lunch spots are available along the shoreline of the lake, but limited legal camping options exist due to the rocky, volcanic nature of the shoreline. Nevertheless, Round Lake is a must-see on any Tahoe hiker's list.

Driving:

   Refer to the Big Meadow Trailhead driving directions on page 97.

Need to Know:

In the early summer months, mosquitos tend to be thick in this area. Bring insect repellent or netting if bothered by the swarming masses.

Alternate Routes:

Round Lake can also be reached from the Lake Valley Trail originating from the end of South Upper Truckee Road in Christmas Valley. From the trailhead, the route climbs 1,500 feet over 3.5 miles but offers a beautiful hike through a major glacial valley that largely contributed to the formation of Lake Tahoe's South Shore.

Dardanelles Lake

Destinations	Distance From Start
Big Meadow Jct.	0.4 MI
Dardanelles Jct.	2.0
Dardanelles Lake	3.4
Round Trip	6.8

Elevation Start: 7,300' End: 7,760' Gain: 460'
Time: 3.5 to 6 hours Difficulty: Moderate

Best for: Day Hike, Overnight

Description:

A gorgeous lake tucked beneath granite cliffs and featuring a sandy shoreline, Dardanelles Lake is a gem in the Meiss Country Roadless Area. Start this hike from the Big Meadow Trailhead, initially following signs for Round Lake. The trail continues for 2.0 miles, climbing up and over a ridge separating Big Meadow from Round and Dardanelles Lakes where it intersects with the Lake Valley Trail.

At this junction, rather than continuine on to Round Lake, bear right toward Dardanelles Lake for just 0.2 miles. Keep your eyes peeled for a junction crossing the stream to the left, as the sign has been missing or damaged the past few summers. After the junction, the trail is well marked as it winds it way westward toward Dardanelles Lake for the next 1.2 miles.

The trail concludes on the eastern shore of Dardanelles, turning into a network of social trails that weave through different campsites scattered around the lake. Spend some time exploring the various islets and peninsulas protruding from the shoreline.

Driving:

Refer to the Big Meadow Trailhead driving directions on page 97.

Need to Know:

-Please practice Leave No Trace Ethics (pages 13-14) to protect the lake from overuse and abuse that may result in future restrictions.

-Observe and obey all fire restrictions that may be in effect. See information on page 13.

Alternate Routes:

Dardanelles Lake can also be reached from the Lake Valley Trail originating from the end of South Upper Truckee Road in Christmas Valley. From the trailhead, the route climbs 1,200 feet over 4.0 miles.

Waterhouse Peak Ridge Traverse

Destinations	Distance From Start
Big Meadow Jct.	0.4 MI
West Summit (unnamed)	3.0
Waterhouse Peak	4.0
Round Trip	8.0

Elevation Start: 7,300' End: 9,497' Gain: 2,197'
Time: 3.5 to 6 hours Difficulty: Hard

Best for: Day Hike, Peakbagging

Description:

A mecca for backcountry skiers in the Winter, Waterhouse Peak is often overlooked in the summer months. With unique views of Hope Valley, Carson Pass, and ranges south of Lake Tahoe, Waterhouse Peak is a rewarding hike any month of the year. This route describes a traverse of the entire ridge line from Big Meadow, but shorter routes are possible (see end of entry). From the Big Meadow Trailhead, cross Highway 89 toward the Round Lake/Scott's Lake junction. Continue toward Scott's Lake a short distance before leaving the trail in favor of a steep cross-country climb to the left.

This is a steep climb with many obstacles and hazards, and is not recommended for novice hikers. Continue hiking uphill until you gain the ridge

101

line after approximately 800 feet of elevation gain. Once you've gained the ridge, continue to hike uphill to the east. The first peak to the west of Waterhouse Peak can be avoided by staying on the south side of the ridge line and maintaining a steady elevation. After approximately 3.2 miles of hiking, you arrive at a small flat saddle between the two peaks.

From this saddle, continue a straight shot uphill to the summit of Waterhouse Peak where you will be rewarded with far-reaching views to the south. To return, you have the option of reversing your route back to the Big Meadow Trailhead, or performing a steep, technical downclimb with sections of bushwhacking to Scott's Lake. From Scott's Lake you can follow the well traveled trail back to the Big Meadow Trailhead.

Driving:
Refer to the Big Meadow Trailhead driving directions on page 97.

Need to Know:
-This ridge traverse requires almost entirely off-trail hiking. Familiarize yourself with the route and terrain before attempting this hike.
-When off-trail, leave as little impact as possible, taking care to avoid trampling fragile high-elevation plant life.

Alternate Routes:
Another cross-country route to the summit can be accomplished from a large turn-out off Highway 89 on the eastern edge of Grass Lake. This is a steep, unrelenting climb up the ridge through thick forest to the summit of Waterhouse Peak.

Desolation Wilderness and large glacial valleys as seen from the ridge leading to Waterhouse Peak.

Stevens Peak

Destinations	Distance From Start***
Depart Rim Trail	1.8 MI
Summit Ridge	3.7
Stevens Peak	4.7
Round Trip	9.4

Elevation Start: 7,300' End: 10,059' Gain: 2,759'
Time: 3.5 to 6 hours   Difficulty: Hard

Best for: Day Hike, Peakbagging
***Distances are approximate, as this hike is almost entirely off trail

Description:

Looming above the Meiss Country Roadless Area, Stevens Peak is a mountain shaped by an awe-inspiring combination of volcanic and glacial influences, creating wide valleys dotted with unique rock formations. To begin this hike from the Big Meadow Trailhead, hike across Highway 89, following the trail toward Round Lake. Continue hiking along the Tahoe Rim Trail for approximately 1.8 miles from the trailhead.

As you begin to climb the ridge that separates Round Lake from Big Meadow, depart from the trail, bearing left instead to follow the long creek drainage. From here, you can either stay low in the valley, following the drainage to the base of Stevens Peak, then climb the northern flank leading to the summit. Or, you may climb the ridge directly above Round Lake, taking care to avoid the cliffs on the western slope. Follow the ridge southeast to the summit of Stevens Peak. Refer to the map on page 96 for a view of these routes.

From the trailhead, it is approximately 4.7 miles to the summit of Stevens Peak. From the summit you are rewarded with spectacular views of Lake Tahoe, Desolation Wilderness, Hope Valley, and the seemingly endless Sierra Nevada range to the south. From here, you can either retrace your steps back to the trailhead, or continue an exciting ridge traverse to Red Lake Peak to the south (Page 107).

Driving:

Refer to the Big Meadow Trailhead driving directions on page 97.

Need to Know:
-This ridge traverse requires almost entirely off-trail hiking. Familiarize yourself with the route and terrain before attempting this hike.
-When off-trail, leave as little impact as possible, taking care to avoid trampling fragile high-elevation plant life.

Alternate Routes:
Another cross-country route to the summit can be accomplished from the south in combination with Red Lake Peak from the Carson Pass Trailhead on Highway 88. See page 107 for details.

Meiss Meadow

Destinations	Distance From Start
Dardanelles Jct.	2.0 MI
Round Lake	2.5
Meiss Meadow	4.9
Round Trip	9.8

Elevation Start: 7,300'   End: 8,380'   Gain: 1,080'
Time: 4.5 to 6 hours   Difficulty: Moderate

Best for: Day Hike

Description:
An absolutely gorgeous alpine meadow restored from its days used for cattle grazing, Meiss Meadow offers a sweeping verdant landscape surrounded by inspiring peaks. To reach this gem from the Big Meadow Trailhead, hike southbound on the Tahoe Rim Trail, following signs for Round Lake. Reaching Round Lake after 2.5 miles of hiking, the terrain starts to transform from dense forest into the more open, grassy forest typical of the transition zones between mountain and meadow.

The trail climbs 300 feet over the next 2.4 miles, winding through transitional forest and crossing several seasonal streams. At the edge of the meadow, the trail intersects with the Pacific Crest Trail after 4.9 miles of hiking, bringing you to Meiss Meadow. This vast expanse stretches for approximately 1.5 miles from north to south, leaving plenty of room for exploration. To the south of this junction, an old cabin and outbuilding still exist from the cattle grazing days of the meadow, with educational signage describing the history of the area.

Driving:

Refer to the Big Meadow Trailhead driving directions on page 97.

Need to Know:

-Because of the cattle history in this meadow, it is strongly recommended that you filter any water drawn from the Upper Truckee River running through the meadow.

Alternate Routes:

Meiss Meadow can also be reached by a much shorter 2.9 mile route from Carson Pass (Page 108).

Showers Lake

Destinations	Distance From Start
Round Lake	2.5 MI
Meiss Meadow	4.9
Showers Lake	7.0
Round Trip	14.0

Elevation Start: 7,300'   End: 8,650'   Gain: 1,350'
Time: 7 to 9 hours   Difficulty: Moderate

Best for: Day Hike, Overnight

Description:

One of this author's favorite lakes in the Tahoe basin, Showers Lake sits perched on an 8,600' foot bench overlooking the Upper Truckee River Valley leading to Lake Tahoe. To reach this lake from the Big Meadow Trailhead, hike southbound on the Tahoe Rim Trail, following signs for Round Lake. Reaching the Dardanelles Lake junction after 2.0 miles, bear left toward Round Lake and Meiss Meadow.

Continue hiking past Round Lake toward the junction with the PCT for an additional 2.9 miles as the trail weaves through grassy forest. At the Meiss Meadow junction, the Tahoe Rim Trail merges with the 2,650 mile Pacific Crest Trail. Bear right at this junction following the sign post for Showers Lake. The trail continues to wind through the meadow, crossing the Upper Truckee River and its side creeks several times before beginning to climb up to the Showers Lake bench.

This section of hike is best enjoyed in the early summer months when spectacular wildflower blooms paint the hillside in vibrant colors. In good snow years, the wildflowers just prior to Showers Lake have been known to grow chest high and taller! The section of PCT just north of Showers Lake is also worth exploring, as it is often referred to as the "Miracle Mile" because of its impressive wildflower displays.

2.1 miles from the TRT/PCT junction, the trail arrives at the southern shore of Showers Lake. Campsites are plentiful and obvious around much of the lakeshore. Just a few hundred yards east of the lake, you can find inspiring vistas of the Upper Truckee River Valley, as well as the cliff bands above Round Lake and Meiss Meadow.

Driving:
Refer to the Big Meadow Trailhead driving directions on page 97.

Need to Know:
-Obey and respect all fire restrictions that may be in place (see page 13 for details).

Alternate Routes:
Showers Lake can also be reached from the Carson Pass Trailhead off Highway 88 for a shorter 5.0 mile one-way hike. Additionally, you have the option of hiking southbound from Echo Summit for 8.3 miles of beautiful ridge line hiking (refer to map for details).

Red Lake Peak from the summit of Stevens Peak.

Red Lake Peak

Destinations	Distance From Start***
Carson Pass	1.2 MI
Red Lake Peak	2.6
Round Trip	5.2

Elevation Start: 8,560' End: 10,063' Gain: 1,503'
Time: 2.5 to 4 hours Difficulty: Moderate

Best for: Day Hike, Peakbagging
***Distances are approximate, as off-trail distances can vary

Description:

A surprisingly attainable 10,000+ foot peak, Red Lake Peak looms over Hope Valley with its stunning volcanic rock outcroppings on the summit block. Begin your hike from the Carson Pass North Trailhead on Highway 88, hiking northbound on the Pacific Crest Trail as it climbs to the Carson Pass saddle. After approximately 1.2 miles of hiking and an elevation gain of 250 feet, you will arrive at the top of Carson Pass where the small tarn to the left of the trail serves as the headwaters of the Upper Truckee River.

At the saddle of Carson Pass, bear right off trail, beginning your cross-country ascent of the summit. Stay along the ridge line for approximately 1.4 miles as you continue to gain 1,200+ feet of elevation. Take care to watch your step and avoid trampling any high elevation flora. The final ridge to the summit bears left among volcanic rock formations bringing you to the summit block.

The actual summit of Red Lake Peak requires a very hazardous and technical Class 3/4 climb up a crumbling volcanic rock formation. For most hikers, the fifteen feet below the true summit can be considered "good enough." From the summit, you may continue northbound along the ridge to bag Stevens Peak, or return down the ridge you ascended to return to the trailhead.

Driving:
Refer to the Carson Pass Trailhead driving directions on page 97.

Need to Know:
-Familiarize yourself with the route and terrain before attempting this hike, as it does involve off-trail hiking
-When off-trail, leave as little impact as possible, taking care to avoid trampling fragile high-elevation plant life.

Alternate Routes:
Red Lake Peak can be reached from the north as a combination hike with Stevens Peak from the Big Meadow Trailhead (page 103).

Meiss Meadow

Destinations	Distance From Start
Carson Pass	1.2 MI
Meiss Meadow TRT Junction	2.9
Round Trip	5.8

Elevation Start: 8,560' End: 8,380' Gain: -180'
Time: 2.5 to 4 hours   Difficulty: Moderate

Best for: Day Hike

Description:

A vast expanse of stunning high alpine meadow and meandering river, the Meiss Meadow Roadless Area isn't to be overlooked on any hiker's list of Tahoe destinations. To access Meiss Meadow from the Carson Pass Trailhead, hike northbound on the Pacific Crest Trail. As you follow the trail up to the Carson Pass Saddle, you are rewarded with stunning views of Elephant's Back, Round Top, Caples Lake, and Kirkwood Ski Resort to the south.

Once reaching the saddle and the headwaters of the Upper Truckee River, the trail begins to descend through open, volcanic terrain into the meadow floor some 500 feet below. Seasonal waterfalls can be found spilling out of the various narrow slots and canyons that funnel down from the summit of Red Lake Peak. You will reach the meadow valley after approximately 2.0 miles of hiking, with the junction to the Tahoe Rim Trail and the center of Meiss Meadow an additional 0.9 miles down the trail.

An old house and cattle grazing structure still exist on the meadow's edge with educational signage depicting the history of the area. Several streams wind through the area, as well as Meiss Lake and Four Lakes (see map on page 96). After 2.9 miles of hiking, the trail joins with the Tahoe Rim Trail where you may either branch right to Round Lake and Big Meadow, or continue straight to Showers Lake and ultimately Echo Summit.

Driving:

Refer to the Carson Pass Trailhead driving directions on page 97.

Need to Know:

-Because of the cattle history in this meadow, it is strongly recommended that you filter any water drawn from the Upper Truckee River running through the meadow.

Alternate Routes:

Meiss Meadow can also be reached from the Big Meadow Trailhead with a 4.9 mile one-way hike. Meiss Meadow is also accessible from an area known as Schneider Cow Camp off Highway 88 for a 4.0 mile one way hike. To reach this trailhead, continue past the Carson Pass Trailhead on Highway 88 for an additional 2.9 miles before turning right on Schneider Cow Camp Rd. (Forest Service Rd 10N13). This is a rough dirt road.

Stevens Peak via Red Lake Peak

Destinations	Distance From Start***
Carson Pass	1.2 MI
Red Lake Peak	2.6
Stevens Peak	4.0
Round Trip	8.0

Elevation Start: 8,560' End: 10,059' Gain: 1,499'
Time: 4 to 7 hours Difficulty: Hard

Best for: Day Hike, Peakbagging
***Distances are approximate, as off-trail distances can vary

Description:

Standing tall above Hope Valley and Meiss Meadow, Stevens Peak offers sweeping panoramic views of the Sierra Nevada south of Lake Tahoe. These directions describe the route to Stevens Peak when combined with an ascent of Red Lake Peak. Beginning from the Carson Pass Trailhead on Highway 88, hike northbound on the Pacific Crest Trail to the saddle of Carson Pass for 1.2 miles. At the saddle of Carson Pass, bear right off trail, beginning your cross-country ascent of the summit. Stay along the ridge line for approximately 1.4 miles as you continue to gain 1,200+ feet of elevation.

The initial 2.6 miles take you to the rocky, spired summit of Red Lake Peak. To reach Stevens Peak, continue traversing the ridge northbound, at first descending 400 feet through stunted White Bark pine. There is a faint path along the ridge that weaves through the rocky volcanic formations, and occasionally requires you to down-climb to the west side of the ridge.

The final ascent to Stevens Peak is a steep climb, scrambling through loose rock before gaining the summit ridge. Bear right on the ridge to reach the summit proper. At the top you are rewarded with fantastic views of the surrounding peaks and valleys. Returning to the trailhead simply requires reversing your route along the ridge. It may be possible to down-climb to Meiss Meadow and follow the PCT back. However, keep in mind that cliff bands exist and will not be shown on the topo map if they are less than 80 feet in height. Use caution on the descent.

Driving:

Refer to the Carson Pass Trailhead driving directions on page 97.

Need to Know:

-Familiarize yourself with the route and terrain before attempting this hike as it does involve off-trail hiking
-When off-trail, leave as little impact as possible, taking care to avoid trampling fragile high-elevation plant life.

Alternate Routes:

Stevens Peak can also be reached from the Big Meadow Trailhead as described on page 103.

Showers Lake

Destinations	Distance From Start
Carson Pass	1.2 MI
Meiss Meadow TRT Junction	2.9
Shower Lake	5.0
Round Trip	10.0

Elevation Start: 8,560' End: 8,650' Net Gain: 90'
Time: 5 to 7 hours Difficulty: Moderate

Best for: Day Hike, Overnight

Description:

Perched upon a small 8,600' bench in the shadow of Little Round Top, Showers Lake offers stunning wildflowers and sweeping views of the Upper Truckee River Valley. Begin your hike from the Carson Pass Trailhead, hiking northbound on the Pacific Crest Trail. The initial 2.9 miles of the hike take you up and over Carson Pass, following the headwaters of the Upper Truckee River as it descends into Meiss Meadow.

As the trail winds through Meiss Meadow, it merges with the Tahoe Rim Trail. Continue straight at this junction following signs for Showers Lake. Passing a small unnamed lake, the trail begins to climb through shaded forest and open wildflower bowls on the way to the Showers Lake bench. After particularly heavy winters, the wildflowers in the final bowl before Showers Lake have been known to grow over head.

After 300 feet of climbing in the last mile, the trail delivers you to the southern shore of Showers Lake. As you continue along the shoreline, abundant camping sites are apparent. Spend time exploring the shoreline, as well as the spectacular views of the valley only a few hundred yards east of the lake. Showers Lake also acts as a good access point for Little Round Top and can act as a stopping point for a nice through-hike from Carson Pass to Echo Summit.

Driving:
Refer to the Carson Pass Trailhead driving directions on page 97.

Need to Know:
-No overnight permits are required, but please obey and respect any fire restrictions that may be in place (see page 13 for details).

Alternate Routes:
Showers Lake can also be reached from the Big Meadow trailhead (page 105) and from Schneider Cow Camp (refer to page 109).

"Walk away quietly in any direction and taste the freedom of the mountaineer. Camp out among the grasses and gentians of glacial meadows, in craggy garden nooks full of nature's darlings. Climb the mountains and get their good tidings, Nature's peace will flow into you as sunshine flows into trees. The winds will blow their own freshness into you and the storms their energy, while cares will drop off like autumn leaves. As age comes on, one source of enjoyment after another is closed, but nature's sources never fail."

-John Muir

SPOONER SUMMIT TO BIG MEADOW

Driving:

Spooner Summit

From South Lake Tahoe, drive east on Highway 50 toward Carson City for 18.1 miles. As you pass the junction for Highway 28 on the left, you will near the top of Spooner Summit. The trailhead is well-marked on the right side of the highway.

Kingsbury South

From South Lake Tahoe, drive east on Highway 50 toward Carson City. Turn right on State Route 207 (Kingsbury Grade). From SR 207 just before the summit, turn right onto Tramway Drive and follow signs for Heavenly Stage-coach parking lot.

Van Sickle Bi-State Park

From South Lake Tahoe, drive east on Highway 50 toward the Stateline casino area. Turn right on Park Avenue and continue until the road meets the entrance of the park.

High Meadow Trailhead

From South Lake Tahoe, turn onto Al Tahoe Blvd toward Pioneer Trail. Turn right on Pioneer Trail and proceed 0.9 miles to High Meadow Trail and turn left. Follow High Meadow Trail to the top, where it turns into a maintained packed dirt road, ultimately turning to a dead end at the trailhead.

Fountain Place Trailhead

From South Lake Tahoe, drive west on Highway 50 toward the small town of Meyers. Just before Meyers, turn left on Pioneer Trail. Continue on Pioneer Trail for 0.9 miles, then turn right onto Oneidas Street. This street continues as a single-lane paved road known as Fountain Place Rd. Continue on Fountain Place Rd. for 3.9 miles until it dead ends at the locked gate signifying the trailhead.

-These hikes can also be reached by a Forest Service Road off High way 89 going up to the backside of Armstrong Pass. However, due to lack of road maintenance, a four-wheel drive car with high clearance is required for the initial portion of the road. By choosing this starting point, subtract approximately 3.5 miles from the distances reflected by starting at Fountain Place.

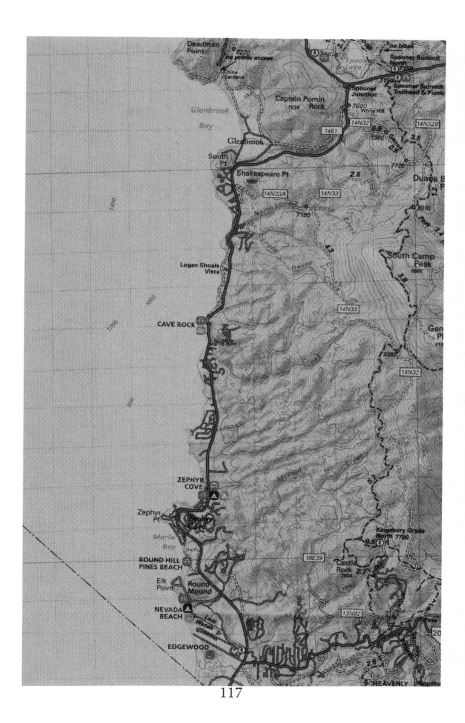

"The Bench"

Destinations	Distance From Start
Genoa Peak Rd.	3.5 MI
The Bench	5.0
Round Trip	10.0

Elevation Start: 7,150'   End: 8,800'   Gain: 1,650'
Time: 5 to 7 hours   Difficulty: Hard

Best for: Day Hike, Peakbagging

Description:

A spectacular vista point aptly named for an actual bench constructed on the ridge, this hike offers astonishing views of Lake Tahoe from the East Shore. Begin this day hike from the Spooner Summit Trailhead on Highway 50, hiking south along the Tahoe Rim Trail. The trail climbs approximately 900 feet over the first 3.5 miles through dense forest, crossing two dirt roads before eventually crossing a third at the junction of Genoa Peak Rd.

This is a good opportunity to take a rest before resuming your hike on the other side of the road, as the final climb to the Bench can be slightly more difficult. The trail climbs through a recovering burn area lush with understory and blooming lupines. After approximately 1.0 mile you emerge above the tree line, yielding panoramic views of Lake Tahoe from the ridge. Continue an additional half mile along the open ridge before encountering "The Bench" on your right.

Take a seat on this excellently crafted wooden bench and enjoy the reward of your five mile hike. To add a few peaks to the day, consider the short traverses to South Camp Peak (next page) and Genoa Peak (page 120).

Driving:

Refer to the Spooner Summit Trailhead directions on page 116.

Need to Know:

-Bring plenty of water with you on this hike, as there are no reliable sources along the way.

-This is a popular trail for mountain bikes, observe right of way signs at the trailhead and know that mountain bikers must yield to hikers.

"The Bench" can also be reached from the Kingsbury North Trailhead by hiking northbound on the Tahoe Rim Trail for approximately 7 miles.

South Camp Peak

Destinations	Distance From Start
Genoa Peak Rd.	3.5 MI
South Camp Peak	5.3
Round Trip	10.6

Elevation Start: 7,150'   End: 8,866'   Gain: 1,716'
Time: 5 to 7 hours   Difficulty: Hard

Best for: Day Hike, Peakbagging

Description:

An unassuming, often overlooked peak, South Camp Peak offers stunning views of Lake Tahoe, Mt. Rose, and the Carson Valley. Begin your hike from the Spooner Summit Trailhead, hiking southbound on the Tahoe Rim Trail, essentially following the same route as "The Bench" (previous page). Continue on the Tahoe Rim Trail past Genoa Peak Road.

As with the hike to "The Bench," you will emerge above the tree line after hiking approximately 4.6 miles. Immediately bear left off trail, hiking cross-country through forest for an additional 0.7 miles toward the summit. Just prior to the actual summit the route opens up into rocky terrain above tree line, finally allowing you to take in the 360 degree views.

Driving:

Refer to the Spooner Summit Trailhead directions on page 116.

Need to Know:

-Bring plenty of water with you on this hike, as there are no reliable sources along the way.
-As with all routes that take you cross-country, familiarize yourself with the route and the map.

Alternate Routes:

A shorter approach might be taken by following Genoa Peak Road for the distance between your first crossing and your second crossing (2nd crossing being at 3.5 miles). This route cuts approximately one mile off the hike, but also forces you to share the road with off-road vehicles. See map on page 117 for reference.

Genoa Peak

Destinations	Distance From Start
Genoa Peak Rd.	3.5 MI
Genoa Peak	6.6
Round Trip	13.2

Elevation Start: 7,150' End: 9,150' Gain: 2,000'
Time: 5 to 7 hours Difficulty: Hard

Best for: Day Hike, Peakbagging

Description:

One of Lake Tahoe's most prominent peaks on the East Shore, Genoa Peak affords brilliant views across Lake Tahoe into Desolation Wilderness and sweeping views of the Carson Valley to the east. Approaching from the north, begin your hike from the Spooner Summit Trailhead and hike southbound on the Tahoe Rim Trail, following the route for "The Bench" (page 118).

To "The Bench," the trail totals 5.0 miles and gains 1,650 feet of elevation. After pausing for a rest, continue southbound on the Tahoe Rim Trail until it starts to descend back into the trees. Stay on the ridge as much as possible without losing more than 150-200 feet of elevation. As the trail begins to descend, you will leave the trail in favor of maintaining elevation, bearing southeast. After only a short distance off-trail you will re-encounter Genoa Peak Rd.

Continue following the road and the obvious path to the summit by bearing left at the junction that leads to the summit. This road also acts a service road for electrical/communications equipment on the summit. From the time you leave the trail to the summit, you will gain approximately 600 additional feet of elevation.

Driving:

Refer to the Spooner Summit Trailhead directions on page 116.

Need to Know:

-Bring plenty of water with you on this hike, as there are no reliable sources along the way.

-As with all routes that take you cross-country, familiarize yourself with the route and the map.

Additional Routes:

As with South Camp Peak, a shorter approach can be taken by following Genoa Peak Rd rather than the Tahoe Rim Trail. This can be done from either the Spooner Summit Trailhead or Kingsbury North Trailhead. Refer to the map on page 117 to see the route.

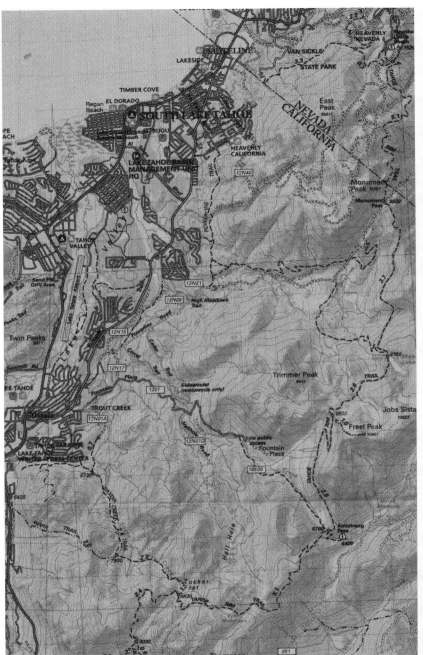

The Carson Range dividing Lake Tahoe and the Carson Valley seen from Monument Peak.

Monument Peak

Destinations	Distance From Start
East Peak Lake	1.6 MI
Monument Peak	4.0
Round Trip	8.0

Elevation Start: 7,520'   End: 10,067'   Gain: 2,547'
Time: 4 to 6 hours   Difficulty: Hard

Best for: Day Hike, Peakbagging

Description:

  Located within the Heavenly Ski Resort boundary, Monument Peak offers towering panoramic views from just above 10,000 feet. This hike begins from the Kingsbury South Trailhead of the Tahoe Rim Trail, but spends little time actually on the Rim Trail. Instead, you will be following Heavenly service roads and social trails the majority of the hike. Heavenly operates under a permit from the US Forest Service, making their service roads completely open to public use. From the trailhead, hike southbound gaining elevation immediately on the service roads.

As a general rule before reaching East Peak Lake, bear uphill and to the left at any road junction you encounter. After approximately 1.6 miles and gaining 1,100' of elevation you arrive at the shore of a water retention basin known as East Peak Lake (do not drink the water in this lake). Continue hiking uphill with Monument Peak in sight. After 3.8 miles of hiking from the trailhead you will arrive just below the summit on a relatively flat road. Break from the road, bearing left for your final summit push over sandy terrain and boulder fields leading to the peak.

Driving:
Refer to the Kingsbury South Trailhead directions on page 116.

Need to Know:
-Bring plenty of water on this sun-exposed, steep hike.
-Yield to any vehicles or heavy equipment traveling on service roads.

Alternate Routes:
For the beginning hiker, it is possible to take the Heavenly Gondola and an additional ski lift to the top of the mountain, turning this into a short 15 minute hike to the summit.

Star Lake

Destinations	Distance From Start
Monument Pass	5.1 MI
Star Lake	8.8
Round Trip	17.6

Elevation Start: 7,520' End: 9,100' Gain: 1,580'
Time: 8 to 10 hours   Difficulty: Hard/Strenuous

Best for: Day Hike, Overnight, Peakbagging

Description:
As one of the highest lakes in the Lake Tahoe basin, the appropriately named Star Lake lies perfectly situated beneath towering Job's Sister at 9,100'.

124

Star Lake at Dusk

To reach Star Lake from the Kingsbury South Trailhead, hike southbound on the well-marked Tahoe Rim Trail. Seasonal water is available on this portion of the hike in a creek draining from Heavenly's Mott Canyon. You will want plenty of water on this long 5.1 mile, sun-exposed trek up and over Monument Pass.

Once at Monument Pass, the trail begins to mellow and only climbs an additional 300 feet in 3.7 miles. Passing through forests of Hemlock, Western White Pine, and Whitebark Pine you will find yourself at the northern shore of Star Lake after hiking 8.8 miles from the trailhead. If camping overnight, a plethora of camping options exist on most shores, save for the southern shoreline. Star Lake acts as an ideal base camp to hike Freel Peak, Job's Sister, and Job's Peak, all well over 10,000 feet. However, if planning Star Lake as a day hike only, be sure to filter water from the lake before beginning your return trip.

Driving:
Refer to the Kingsbury South Trailhead directions on page 116.

Need to Know:
-Bring plenty of water on this sun-exposed, steep hike.
-Woodfires are sometimes allowed depending on seasonal fire conditions. Obey and respect all fire restrictions by checking with the LTBMU before your trip (page 13).

Alternate Routes:
Star Lake can also be reached from the High Meadow Trailhead (page 128) in 7.8 miles and from the Fountain Place Trailhead (page 136) in 8.0 miles.

Van Sickle Connector

Destinations	Distance From Start
Waterfall Vista	1.3 MI
Tahoe Rim Trail	3.7
Round Trip	7.4

Elevation Start: 6,440'   End: 7,760'   Gain: 1,320'
Time: 3.5 to 5 hours   Difficulty: Moderate

Best for: Day Hike

Description:

A recent addition connecting the nation's first bi-state park with the Tahoe Rim Trail, the Van Sickle Connector offers a perfect day-hike for all abilities. Begin your hike from the main parking lot of the Van Sickle Bi-State Park, following signs for the Tahoe Rim Trail. The newly constructed trail weaves through the recovering burn area of the 2002 Gondola Fire, yielding spectacular verdant growth in the early summer.

For beginning hikers, a pleasant waterfall serves as a rewarding destination after 1.3 miles of hiking and 600 feet of elevation gain. From the waterfall, the trail continues to climb at a moderate rate, eventually moving out of the burn zone into shaded forest providing relief from the sun. After 3.7 miles of hiking, you will arrive at the junction with the 170-mile Tahoe Rim Trail. A worthwhile vista marked at elevation 7,777' awaits you at this junction.

From here you have the choice of returning back down the trail, or for the ambitious and athletic hiker, continuing up to Monument Peak (page 123). In either case, the Van Sickle connector offers terrain and views for all groups looking for a great introduction to Lake Tahoe.

Driving:

Refer to the Van-Sickle Bi-State Park directions on page 116.

Need to Know:

This is a popular trail with mountain bikers as well. Familiarize yourself with trail etiquette and right of way rules at the trailhead, or on page 19.

High Meadows via Cold Creek

Destinations	Distance From Start
High Meadows	3.6 MI
Round Trip	7.2

Elevation Start: 6,640'   End: 7,840'   Gain: 1,200'
Time: 3.5 to 5 hours   Difficulty: Moderate

Best for: Day Hike

Description:

A relatively well-kept secret in comparison with many of South Lake Tahoe's area trails, the Cold Creek Trail to High Meadows provides wonderful creekside hiking for the duration of the hike. Starting from the High Meadows Trailhead, follow the trail to the left of the parking lot, rather than following the dirt road behind the locked gate. After a short distance you will cross over Cold Creek, encountering a junction to the "Powerline Trail." Bear right at the junction, following the trail upstream.

From here the route is straightforward and easy to follow the entire 3.6 mile distance to High Meadows. Several points on the trail offer shaded, cool resting spots along the verdant banks of Cold Creek. Keep an eye and ear out for mountain bikers, as the 1,200 feet of elevation gain/loss make this a popular singletrack trail.

Once you arrive at High Meadows, enjoy the network of creeks and abundant high alpine flora. From High Meadows, you have the option of continuing up to Star Lake via the the Star Lake Connector (next page), or following the dirt road to Monument Pass.

Driving:

Refer to the High Meadows Trailhead directions on page 116.

Need to Know:

This is a popular trail with mountain bikers as well. Familiarize yourself with trail etiquette and right of way rules at the trailhead, or on page 19.

Star Lake via High Meadow

Destinations	Distance From Start
High Meadows	3.6 MI
Star Lake	7.8
Round Trip	15.6

Elevation Start: 6,640'   End: 9,100'   Gain: 2,460'
Time: 7.5 to 9 hours   Difficulty: Hard

Best for: Day Hike, Overnight

Description:

Thanks to a newly constructed trail connecting High Meadows to the Tahoe Rim Trail, the magnificent Star Lake is more accessible than ever before. Beginning from the High Meadows Trailhead off Pioneer Trail, follow the same route for High Meadows via the Cold Creek Trail (previous page). During the initial portion of the hike you gain 1,200 feet of elevation over 3.6 miles. Upon reaching the dirt road in High Meadows, bear right, following the road south. After 0.6 miles, bear left at a junction, signed only by a fading laminate sign by the Forest Service.

This wide dirt path soon becomes a distinct trail climbing to Star Lake. As you gain an additional 1,200 feet of elevation, be sure to stop and look over your shoulder for gorgeous views of Lake Tahoe. From the junction in High Meadows the trail continues 3.6 miles, crossing several refreshing streams, before meeting the Tahoe Rim Trail at the southern edge of Star Lake. Enjoy the grassy and sandy shoreline of Star Lake before your return hike, or discover one of the numerous camp sites around the lake if on an overnight trip.

Driving:

Refer to the High Meadows Trailhead directions on page 116.

Need to Know:

Familiarize yourself with trail etiquette and right of way rules at the trailhead, or on page 19.

Alternate Routes:

Star Lake can also be reached from the Kingsbury South Trailhead (page 124) and the Fountain Place Trailhead (page 136).

"As long as I live, I'll hear waterfalls and birds and winds sing. I'll interpret the rocks, learn the language of flood, storm, and the avalanche. I'll acquaint myself with the glaciers and wild gardens, and get as near the heart of the world as I can."

-John Muir

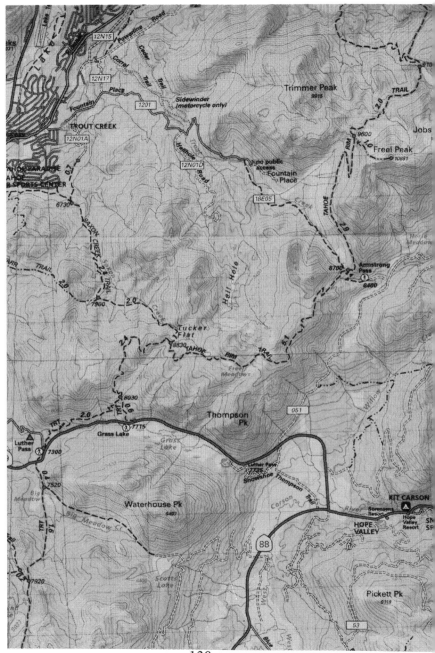

130

Lake Tahoe from the summit of Trimmer Peak

Trimmer Peak

Destinations	Distance From Start
Armstrong Pass	3.6 MI
Freel Saddle	6.5
Trimmer Peak	7.8
Round Trip	15.6

Elevation Start: 7,680'   End: 9,915'   Gain: 2,235'
Time: 7.5 to 9 hours   Difficulty: Hard

Best for: Day Hike, Peakbagging

Description:

Quite possibly one of the least known peaks in the Tahoe area, even by locals, Trimmer Peak stands 200 feet taller than the ever-popular Mt. Tallac, while offering views of Lake Tahoe to rival any peak in the basin. Beginning from the trailhead at the top of Fountain Place Road, hike the winding Armstrong Pass Connector trail through dense forest, gaining 1,020' in 3.6 miles. At

131

the junction atop Armstrong Pass, bear left on the Tahoe Rim Trail following signs for Star Lake.

The trail continues to climb an additional 900 feet over 2.9 miles, yielding spectacular views of Pyramid Peak and the American River Valley. This section of trail still remains one of the author's favorite in the basin for its beauty and relative solitude. Climbing two large switchbacks, you arrive at the 9,600' saddle that serves as the departure point to climb Freel Peak (next page). Because Freel Peak is the biggest draw along this trail, Trimmer Peak sees astonishingly few visitors in comparison.

Rather than continuing on the Tahoe Rim Trail, bear left along the ridge line from the saddle, traversing northbound. The first peak you encounter is a false summit, and will actually require you to lose a few hundred feet of elevation before making the final push to the summit of Trimmer Peak. Use caution in the last few hundred feet before the summit, as Class 3 climbing may be required. Once on the summit, enjoy spectacular views of Lake Tahoe, Desolation Wilderness, High Meadows, and Freel Peak/Job's Sister.

Driving:
Refer to the Fountain Place Trailhead driving directions on page 116.

Need to Know:
-This is a long, sun-exposed hike with steady elevation gain. Bring plenty of water.
-Cross-country travel is required. Be sure to familiarize yourself with the terrain and the map before you hike.

Alternate Routes:
Armstrong Pass can also be reached with a 4WD vehicle from the south as described on page 116. This turns the hike into an approximately 4.5 mile one-way hike.

Freel Peak

Destinations	Distance From Start
Armstrong Pass	3.6 MI
Freel Saddle	6.5
Freel Peak	7.5
Round Trip	15.0

Elevation Start: 7,680' End: 10,881' Gain: 3,201'
Time: 7.5 to 9 hours Difficulty: Strenuous

Best for: Day Hike, Peakbagging

Description:
   With the honor of being the tallest peak in the Lake Tahoe Basin at 10,881 feet, Freel Peak is a challenging, yet incredibly rewarding peak that should be on every Tahoe hiker's bucket list. Beginning from the Fountain Place Trailhead, follow the Armstrong Pass Connector Trail for 3.6 miles to link up with the Tahoe Rim Trail. As Freel Peak consists of constant elevation gain for 7.5 miles, a short 5 minute rest at Armstrong Pass is recommended before continuing on the Rim Trail toward Star Lake.
   Continue climbing to the Freel Saddle, crossing several seasonal streams and winding through two large switchbacks in this 2.9 mile segment. Cresting over Freel Saddle, you are offered a rewarding view of Lake Tahoe, Monument Peak, and High Meadows, with Freel Peak and Job's Sister looming overhead. Take one more rest at the saddle before following the 1.0 mile trail to the summit of Freel Peak.
   This last mile of trail gains over 1,200 feet of elevation, pushing your legs to their limits. For those not used to the altitude, crossing the 10,000 foot line can certainly take its toll. Be sure to bring plenty of food and water to combat altitude sickness. After a long 7.5 miles of climbing over 3,000 feet, enjoy the awe-inspiring panoramic views from the summit of Tahoe's tallest peak. Ambitious hikers can also tackle the summit of Job's Sister, the second highest peak in Tahoe, directly east of Freel Peak.

Driving:
   Refer to the Fountain Place Trailhead driving directions on page 116.

Need to Know:
-When on the final approach to Freel Peak, stay on trail to protect endangered high-altitude plant species.

Alternate Routes:
      A shorter 3.9 mile route up Freel Peak can be managed from the south side of Armstrong Pass, but requires a four-wheel drive vehicle with high clearance. Freel Peak can also be reached from High Meadows or Kingsbury South by following the route to Star Lake and continuing on the Tahoe Rim Trail to the Freel Saddle. Kingsbury South, however, might be better accomplished on an overnight trip by camping at Star Lake.

From Left to Right: Job's Peak, Job's Sister and Freel Peak from the summit of Monument Peak

Job's Sister

Destinations	Distance From Start
Freel Saddle	6.5 MI
Freel Peak	7.5
Job's Sister	8.5
Round Trip	17.0

Elevation Start: 7,680' End: 10,823' Gain: 3,143'**
Time: 8.5 to 11 hours   Difficulty: Strenuous
Best for: Day Hike, Peakbagging

**Net gain from Trailhead. Gross gain by hiking up and over Freel is closer to 4,000'

Description:

As Freel Peak's next door neighbor, Job's Sister is the second tallest peak in the Lake Tahoe basin standing only 58 feet below the summit of Freel. Most hikers tend to combine these two peaks into one challenging day hike. For brevity, refer to the route description for Freel Peak first, as all directions will be the same until the summit of Freel.

After hiking 7.5 miles from Fountain Place to the summit of Freel Peak, begin your descent of the eastern ridge toward Job's Sister. There is a social trail that follows old cable casing for a microwave tower that used to stand atop Freel. Looking at Job's Sister, the trail stays to the left side of the ridge. As you near the base of Job's Sister, the social trail begins to fade into a grove of stunted Whitebark Pine, but all roads lead to the summit at this point. Take care to avoid stepping on any plant life, as the endangered Tahoe Draba lives almost exclusively in this area.

After obtaining the summit of Job's Sister, you must either climb back up and over Freel Peak to get back to the trail, or drop down another social trail into the bowl between the northern slope of the two mountains, following the drainage until it intersects with the Tahoe Rim Trail. From there you must hike the TRT back up to Freel Saddle.

Driving:

Refer to the Fountain Place Trailhead driving directions on page 116.

Need to Know:

-Stay on trail to protect endangered high-altitude plant species. If hiking cross-country, watch your step carefully.

-Familarize yourself with the map and the route before hiking cross-country.

Alternate Routes:

A 4.9 mile route can be managed from the south side of Armstrong Pass, but requires a four-wheel drive vehicle with high clearance. Job's Sister can be reached from High Meadows or Kingsbury South by following the route to Star Lake and continuing on the Tahoe Rim Trail to the Freel Saddle. Hiking from Kingsbury South might be better accomplished on an overnight trip by camping at Star Lake.

Star Lake

Destinations	Distance From Start
Armstrong Pass	3.6 MI
Freel Saddle	6.5
Star Lake	8.5
Round Trip	17.0

Elevation Start: 7,680' End: 9,100' Gain: 1,420'

Time: 8.5 to 11 hours Difficulty: Hard

Best for: Day Hike, Peakbagging, Overnight

Description:

As described on pages 124 and 128, Star Lake is a wonderful back-country lake with a multitude of camping options. From the Fountain Place Trailhead, hike 3.6 miles up the Armstrong Pass Connector to join the Tahoe Rim Trail. Bear left at the junction following the sign post for Star Lake. The trail climbs 2.9 miles to the Freel Saddle at 9,600', the high point of your trip to Star Lake.

After taking in the views of Tahoe from the saddle, the trail begins to descend into sandy forest skirting the base of Freel and Job's Sister. Continue following the Tahoe Rim Trail for an additional 2.0 miles, losing aproximately 500 feet of elevation before arriving at the edge of Star Lake. In total, the distance from Fountain Place is 8.5 miles on well-marked trail.

Driving:

Refer to the Fountain Place Trailhead driving directions on page 116.

Need to Know:

-Woodfires are sometimes allowed depending on seasonal fire conditions. Obey and respect all fire restrictions by checking with the LTBMU before your trip (page 13).

Alternate Routes:

A shorter 5.0 mile route can be managed from the south side of Armstrong Pass, but requires a four-wheel drive vehicle with high clearance. Star Lake can also be reached from High Meadows (page 128) and Kingsbury South (page 124).

Index

Equipment needed: 50FT of 2-3mm nylon cord, 2 stuff sacks, 2-3 mini carabiners, 1 small rock sack (made from tough material like cordura)

1. Locate a mature tree at least 50 feet from your campsite. The tree should
   have a sturdy branch 8 to 10 feet in length and 10 to 15 feet off of the
   ground.

2. Place a medium-sized rock inside of a small stuff sack and attach the cord to
   it (mini carabiners work great for this).

3. Throw the weighted end of the cord over the branch, ideally in a spot toward
   the middle of the branch that is also free of smaller branches that may
   snag your cord.

4. Remove the rock sock and attach one of the two equally weighted food sacks
   to that end of the cord. Pull the stuff sack up so that it is about 1-2 feet
   below the branch.

5. Attach the second food sack to the cord as high as you can reach. Wind up
   the remaining length of cord and affix it to the top of the food sack.
   (You can leave a short length of cord with a loop at the end so that it
   dangles just below the bottom of the second food sack, leaving some-
   thing to snag to retrieve the sacks). Push this second food sack up so
   that both bags are at an equal height approximately 10-12 feet off the
   ground. You may have to use a long branch or trekking pole to accomplish this.

6. To retrieve the sacks in the morning use the long branch or your trekking
   pole to snag the loop you left dangling and pull the excess looped cord
   down. Now pull the second food sack down and un-attach it from the
   cord. Next lower the first sack down to the ground and un-attach it
   from the cord. Then pull the cord over the branch, being careful not to
   snag it.

Appendix C - Hike Index by Type
Note: All hikes described in this book are suitable for day hikes. The index below distinguishes between Overnight trips and Peakbagging trips.

Notes

Notes

Notes

About the Author

Aaron Hussmann was born and raised in South Lake Tahoe, California. After studying Psychology with a concentration in Environmental Psychology at Cal Poly San Luis Obispo, he moved back to the glorious Sierra Nevada mountains for an intentional summer of hiking and backpacking that became the basis for this guide. He spends his time enjoying as much of Tahoe's beautiful backyard as possible.

Made in the USA
San Bernardino, CA
05 June 2016